Music Theory
UNTANGLED COURSE

**GRADE 1
SECOND EDITION**

BY JANE STAVRINOUDIS

MUSIC THEORY UNTANGLED COURSE
GRADE 1 - Second Edition

By Jane Stavrinoudis

Untangle the world of music theory with this engaging and accessible resource designed to make learning music theory clear and rewarding for students of all ages and instruments.

With its easy-to-follow lessons, numerous sample questions and exercises, practical answers and video explanations, this book offers a clear, step-by-step approach to understanding music theory concepts.

Whether you're just starting out or preparing for formal theory exams with your preferred major examination body, this book is your key to mastering music theory with confidence.

How to use:

1) For each lesson, watch the short explanation video by clicking on the link OR by scanning the QR code. Have your concept sheets open so that you know where to find the concepts discussed in the video.

2) Work through the online quiz for that lesson and refer to your concept sheets as you go.

3) Complete the exercises in the worksheets for that lesson and refer to your concept sheets as you go.

4) Mark your work using the answers and remember that there will sometimes be more than one correct answer.

5) If applicable, you will now be ready to work through practice examinations with your preferred theory examination body.

CONTENTS

Concepts	4-13
Note and rest values	5
Note and rest tree	5
Staves and Barlines	6
Dotted Notes	6
Tuplets	6
Direction of stems	7
Time signatures	7
Beams and flags	7
Tones and semitones	8
Accidentals	8
Note names	9
Leger lines	9
Rhymes for note names	9
Key signatures	10
Scale degree numbers and technical names	10
Semitones in major scales	10
Intervals	10
Tonic triads and their positions ...	11
Transposition	11
Terms and definitions	12

Worksheets	14-49
Lesson 1	15
Lesson 2	18
Lesson 3	22
Lesson 4	26
Lesson 5	30
Lesson 6	34
Lesson 7	38
Lesson 8	41
Lesson 9	47
Answers	50-76
Lesson 1	51
Lesson 2	53
Lesson 3	57
Lesson 4	60
Lesson 5	63
Lesson 6	66
Lesson 7	69
Lesson 8	72
Lesson 9	76
Certificate	77

Grade 1 Music Theory Untangled Course
© 2024 Jane Stavrinoudis. All rights reserved. Unauthorised reproduction is illegal. For more courses and piano sheet music visit the website and subscribe to the YouTube channel for Jane Stavrinoudis Piano

GRADE 1
SECOND EDITION

Music Theory
UNTANGLED COURSE CONCEPTS

BY JANE STAVRINOUDIS

NOTE AND REST VALUES

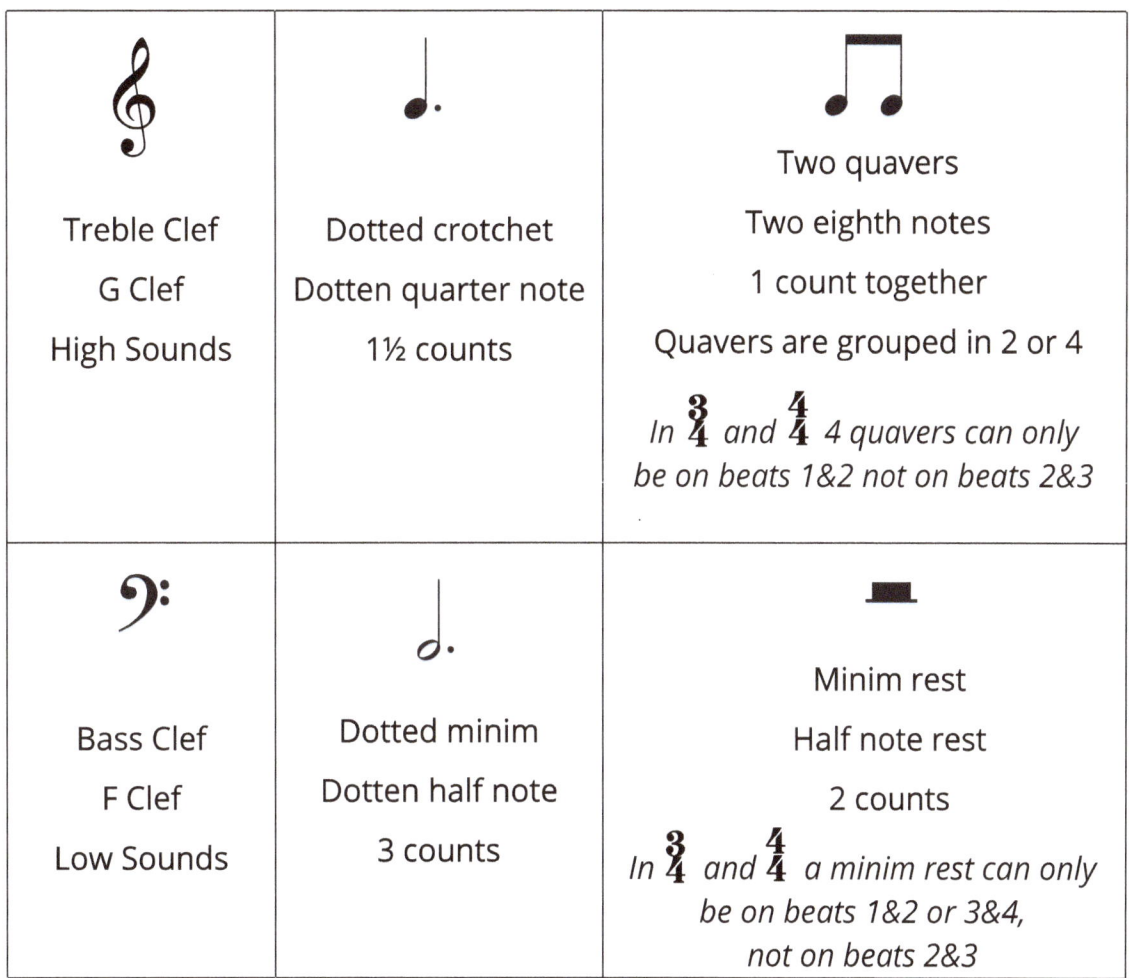

NOTE AND REST TREE

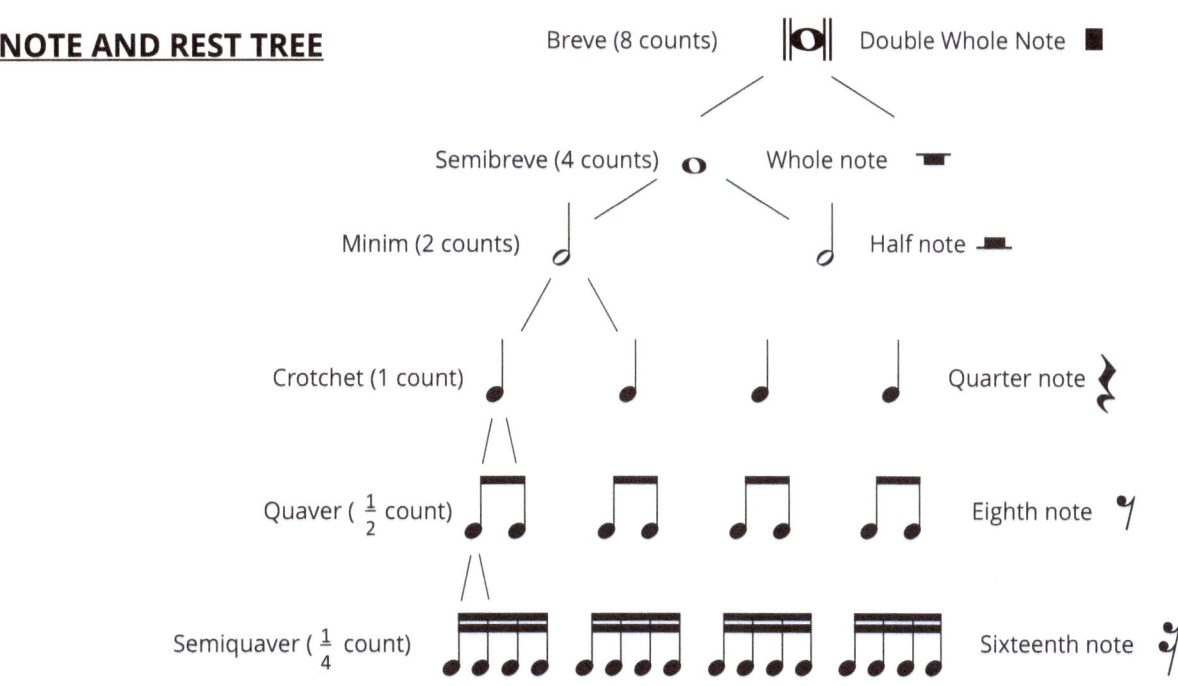

STAVES AND BARLINES

Staff or Stave: a set of five horizontal lines and four spaces where musical notes are written. These lines and spaces represent different musical pitches, with the help of a clef symbol at the beginning of the stave. A clef indicates which pitch each line and space represents.

Barlines: a segment of music bounded by vertical lines called bar lines. A bar or measure is a unit of time in music, representing a specific number of beats. The number of beats in each bar is determined by the time signature. A single barline sets the boundaries for a bar (or measure). A double barline indicates the end of a section. An end barline indicates the end of the music.

DOTTED NOTES

The first dot increases the duration of the original note by half of its original value.

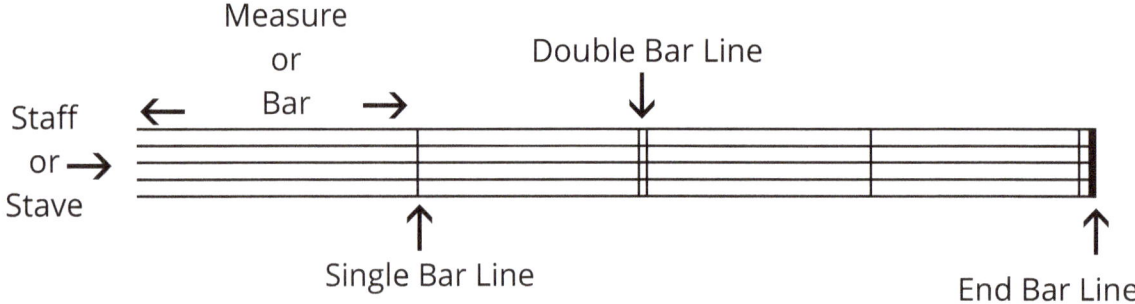

TUPLETS

A tuplet is any rhythm that involves dividing the beat into a different number of equal subdivision from that usually permitted by the time-signature. This is indicated by a number which represents the fraction involved. The notes are also often grouped with a bracket or slur. In Common time quavers would usually be groups of 2 for one beat but a triplet is quavers in a group of 3 but played in the same time as a group of 2.

DIRECTION OF STEMS

When the note head is on the middle line, the stem can go up OR down.

When the note head is above the middle line, the stem will go down on the left.

When the note head is below the middle line, the stem will go up on the right.

TIME SIGNATURES

The **top** number is the **number** of beats in each bar.

The **bottom** number is the *how long* each beat is.

Time Signatures are NOT fractions, just one number below the other.

$\frac{2}{4}$ simple duple time (2 crotchet beats per bar)

$\frac{3}{4}$ simple triple time (3 crotchet beats per bar)

C (common time) or $\frac{4}{4}$ simple quadruple time (4 crotchet beats per bar)

BEAMS AND FLAGS

A beam is a horizontal or diagonal line used to connect the stems of multiple eighth notes (quavers), sixteenth notes (semiquavers), or shorter notes to indicate rhythmic grouping and make musical notation easier to read. A flag is used for individual quavers or semiquavers.

The number of beams corresponds to the number of flags that would be present on the unbeamed notes. For example, eighth notes (quavers) have one beam, and sixteenth notes (semiquavers) have two beams.

Notes joined by a beam usually have all the stems pointing in the same direction (up or down). The average pitch of the notes is used to determine the direction – if the average pitch is below the middle staff-line, the stems and beams usually go above the notehead, otherwise they go below.

The direction of beams usually follows the general direction of the noteheads it groups, slanting down if the noteheads go down, slanting up if the noteheads go up, and level if the first and last notes are the same.

Beams group notes to make it easier to read, and to identify individual beats. In Simple Duple or Quadruple time, beams or flags are used to show each beat clearly. The first note of each group must fall on the beat, not on an off beat. In any simple time sign, beams cannot be used to join beats 2-3.

TONES AND SEMITONES

A semitone is the smallest distance between one note and the very next note. A tone is two semitones.

ACCIDENTALS

In music, an accidental is a note of a pitch that is not a member of the scale or mode indicated by the most recently applied key signature. In musical notation, the sharp, flat, and natural symbols, among others, mark such notes—and those symbols are also called accidentals.

♯ sharp (raise the note by one semitone)

♭ flat (lower the note by one semitone)

♮ natural (cancel the previous sharp or flat)

NOTES NAMES

There are four spaces and five lines in each stave. Check the clef, then count from the lowest note and use the rhyme to work out the letter name of the note. The first letter of each word will give you that note's letter name.

C6
C5
Middle C
C4
C3
C2

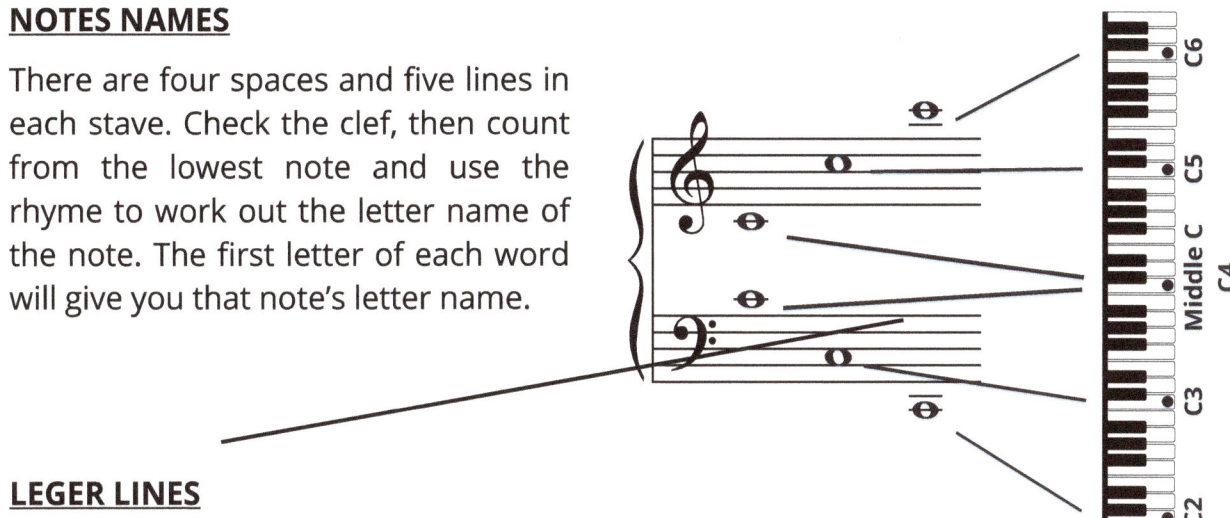

LEGER LINES

A leger line is used to notate pitches above or below the lines and spaces of the regular musical staff. A line slightly longer than the note head is drawn parallel to the staff, above or below, spaced at the same distance as the within the staff.

RHYMES FOR NOTE NAMES

TREBLE CLEF SPACES

F A C E

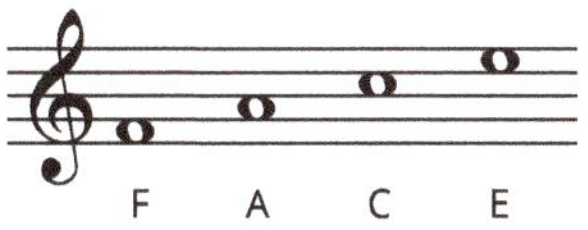

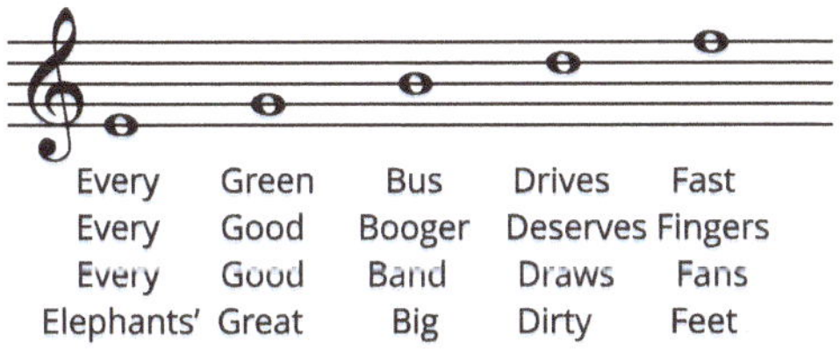

Every Green Bus Drives Fast
Every Good Booger Deserves Fingers
Every Good Band Draws Fans
Elephants' Great Big Dirty Feet

TREBLE CLEF LINES

BASS CLEF SPACES

All Cows Eat Grass

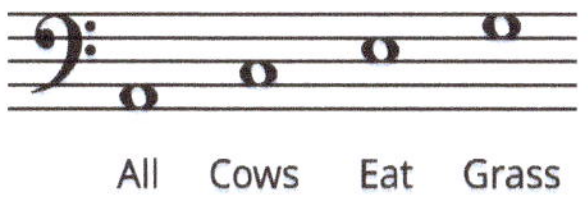

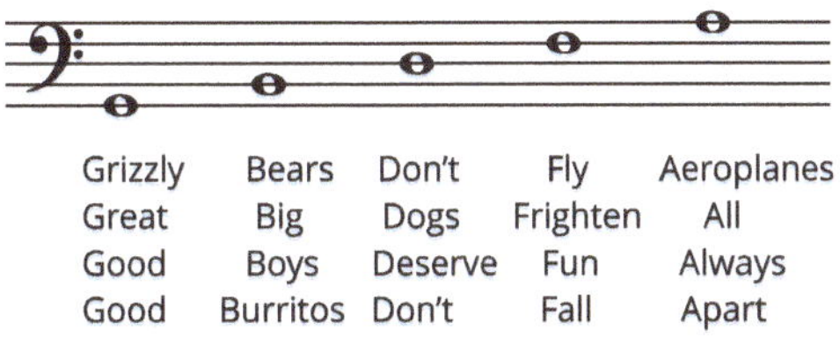

Grizzly Bears Don't Fly Aeroplanes
Great Big Dogs Frighten All
Good Boys Deserve Fun Always
Good Burritos Don't Fall Apart

BASS CLEF LINES

KEY SIGNATURES

A key signature is a set of sharps (♯) or flats (♭) placed together on the staff. Key signatures are generally written immediately after the clef at the beginning of a line of musical notation, although they can appear in other parts of a score.

A key signature designates notes that are to be played higher or lower than the corresponding natural notes and applies through to the end of the piece or up to the next key signature.

C Major

G Major

F Major

SCALE DEGREE NUMBERS AND TECHNICAL NAMES

Note number 1 in the scale is the first note etc

1 = tonic	2 = supertonic	3 = mediant	4 = subdominant
5 = dominant	6 = submediant	7 = leading note	

SEMITONES IN MAJOR SCALES   Are between scale degree numbers 3&4 and 7&8

INTERVALS

The distance between two notes. Count the lowest note as 1, then count up the notes of the scale including the starting and finishing notes. Name the interval the scale degree number you landed on eg 3rd.

When writing an interval above a given note, the given note is the Major key you are in and is also note 1. Count up from that note, write in the interval note, then check the key signature to see if an accidental is needed.

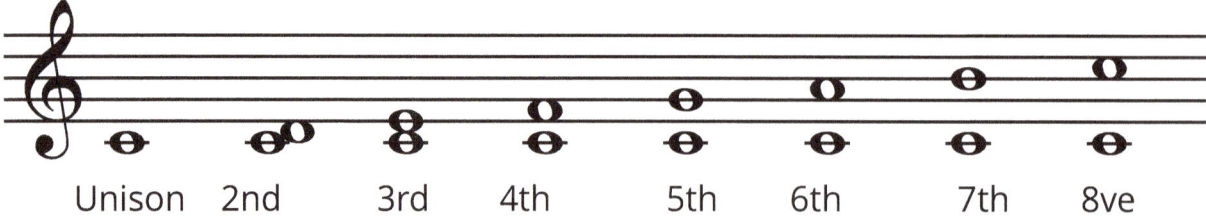
Unison   2nd   3rd   4th   5th   6th   7th   8ve

TONIC TRIADS

A triad is a chord made up of 3 notes: the 1st, 3rd and 5th notes where the first note is the tonic (note number 1) of the scale/key. Can be written with or without the key signature, it will depend on the question. If the key signature is written, then you don't need to worry about accidentals. BUT if the key signature is not written, then you need to add the accidental for the notes that need them that match the key sign.

Arabic Numbers: 1   2   3   4   5   6   7   *used for fingering*

Roman Numbers: I   II   III   IV   V   VI   VII   *used for chords*

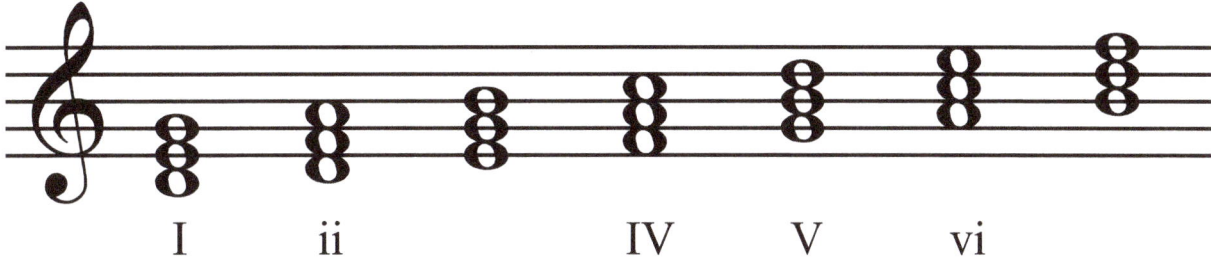

THE THREE PRIMARY TRIADS

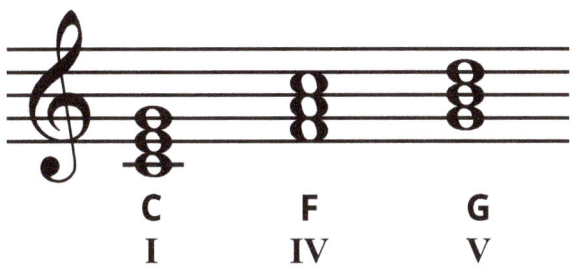

THE THREE POSITIONS

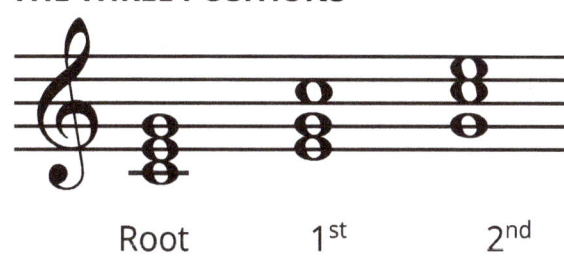

TRANSPOSITION

Shifting a melody either up or down without changing it.

1) Work out the key of the melody, then write in the scale degree numbers under each note.

2) Write in the key signature of the new key, then write in each note to match the scale degree numbers in the new key. Check the question for which way: up or down?

3) Add in all the markings from the original melody.

TERMS AND DEFINITIONS

a	at, to, by, for	
a tempo	return to the former speed	
accelerando	or *accel* - gradually becoming faster	
accent	the note is to be louder, with more attack	♩ >
Adagio	slowly	**Adagio** ♩ = 40
Allegretto	moderately fast	**Allegretto** ♩ = 116
Allegro	lively and fast	**Allegro** ♩ = 120
Andante	at an easy walking pace	**Andante** ♩ = 76-100
cantabile	lyrically, in a singing style	
Capo	beginning	
coda	A section of music added at the end	
crescendo	or *cresc* - gradually becoming louder	⟨
Da, Del	From the	
DC al Fine or *Da Capo al Fine*	from the beginning to *Fine*	
Dal Segno	from the sign	𝄋
Dal Segno al Fine	from the sign to *Fine*	𝄋
decrescendo	or *decresc* - gradually becoming softer	⟩
diminuendo	or *dim* - gradually becoming softer	⟩
Fermata	Pause; lengthen the value of the note or rest	𝄐
Fine	the end of the piece	
forte	loud	*f*
fortissimo	very loud	*ff*
Harmony	a combination of musical sounds	
legato	smoothly, well connected	♫ ♫

Lento	slowly	**Lento** ♩= 45-60
Loco	at normal pitch	
M.M.	Maelzel's Metronome - beats per minute, how fast to play	
Melody	a succession of single sounds	
mezzo	moderately or medium	
mezzo forte	medium loud	*mf*
mezzo piano	medium soft	*mp*
Moderato	at a moderate speed	**Moderato** ♩= 108
Opus	a work or group of works	
ottava bassa	play an octave lower than written	8vb - - - - - - -
piano	soft	*p*
poco	a little	
Presto	very fast	**Presto** ♩= 168-200
rallentando	(or rall) gradually becoming slower	
Repeat sign	Play again	:||
ritardando	(or ritard or rit) gradually becoming slower	
ritenuto	(or riten) held back, immediately becoming slower	
Segno	Sign	
slur	two notes of different pitches smoothly connected	
staccato	short and detached	
Swung	play the quavers unevenly with an underlying triplet feel	
Tempo	speed	
Tenuto (or ten.)	held, play for the full duration of the note	
tie	two notes of same pitch, played once but held for the value of both	

GRADE 1
SECOND EDITION

Music Theory
UNTANGLED COURSE
WORKSHEETS

BY JANE STAVRINOUDIS

LESSON 1 TIME SIGNATURES

Watch this video first:

https://youtu.be/k-ud0yEFAfo

Work through this online quiz:

https://www.flexiquiz.com/SC/N/10a8769b-6c5e-4e6c-b671-e33a6dbd171a

QUESTION 1: What does $\frac{2}{4}$ stand for? _____

QUESTION 2: What does $\frac{3}{4}$ stand for? _____

QUESTION 3: What does $\frac{4}{4}$ stand for? _____

QUESTION 4: What does 𝄴 stand for? _____

QUESTION 5: Draw a line to join the note or rest with its name.

Crotchet rest

Eighth note

Half note

Minim rest

Quarter note

Quaver rest

Semibreve

Semiquaver

Whole bar rest

Grade 1 Music Theory Untangled Course Worksheets

QUESTION 6: Complete these sums. Use numbers for your answers.

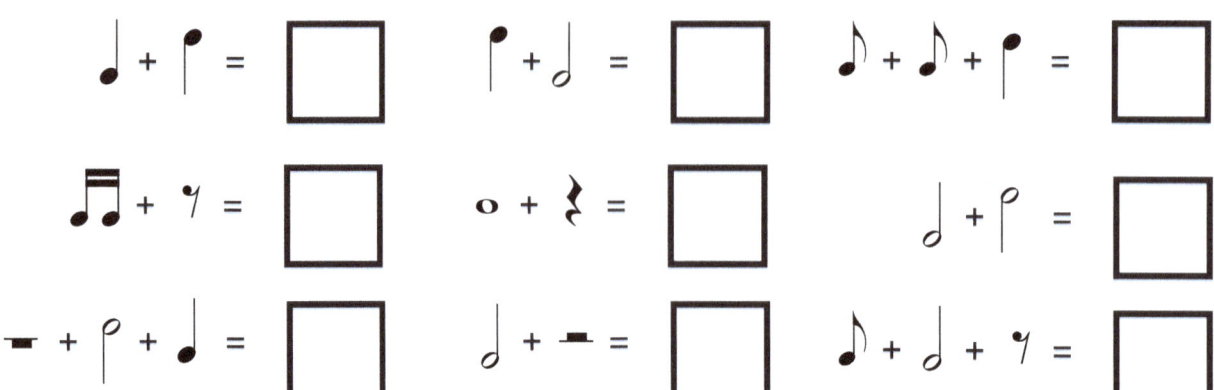

QUESTION 7: Complete each of these bars with crotchets and/or quavers.

QUESTION 8: Complete each of these bars with crotchet rests and/or quaver rests.

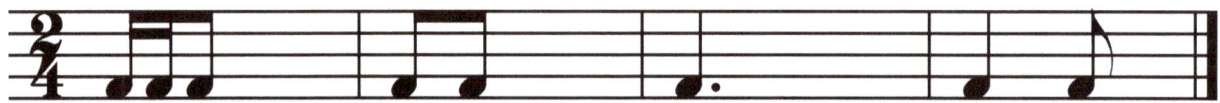

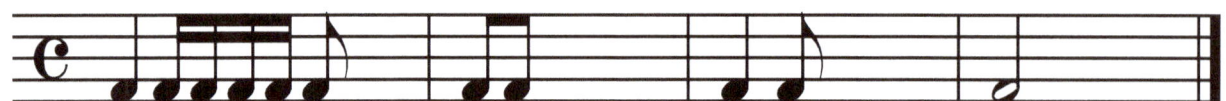

QUESTION 9: Listen to each of the pieces and tick what is the correct time signature?

a) Royal Marines Corp of Drums and Top Secret Drum Corps (The Bands of HM Royal Marines)   https://www.youtube.com/watch?v=x9nmSJ3gesE

   Simple Duple Time ☐   Simple Triple Time ☐   Simple Quadruple Time

b) The Second Waltz (Andre Rieu)
   https://www.youtube.com/watch?v=xtac0FxEfmQ

   Simple Duple Time ☐   Simple Triple Time ☐   Simple Quadruple Time

c) Zorba The Greek Dance   https://www.youtube.com/watch?v=kG12C1oX5Eo

   Simple Duple Time ☐   Simple Triple Time ☐   Simple Quadruple Time

d) Norwegian Wood (The Beatles)
   https://www.youtube.com/watch?v=Y_V6y1ZCg_8

   Simple Duple Time ☐   Simple Triple Time ☐   Simple Quadruple Time

e) Gone Wanderin' (Jackie Greene)
   https://www.youtube.com/watch?v=Ue--c6TcuQE

   Simple Duple Time ☐   Simple Triple Time ☐   Simple Quadruple Time

f) Dancing Queen (ABBA)   https://www.youtube.com/watch?v=xFrGuyw1V8s

   Simple Duple Time ☐   Simple Triple Time ☐   Simple Quadruple Time

LESSON 2 CLEFS, NOTES, STEMS AND BARLINES

Watch this video first:

https://youtu.be/iUg4FvLsKqg

Work through this online quiz:

https://www.flexiquiz.com/SC/N/bc1c0447-aa44-4ef9-8a01-33d408cf6f3a

QUESTION 1: What is this symbol called, and does it notate high or low pitch?

QUESTION 2: What is this symbol called, and does it notate high or low pitch?

QUESTION 3: What is this symbol called, and how long is it in simple time?

QUESTION 4: What is this symbol called, and how long is it in simple time?

QUESTION 5: What is this symbol called, and how long is it in any time?

QUESTION 6: What is this symbol called, and what does it mean?

QUESTION 7: What is this symbol called, and what does it mean?

QUESTION 8: Add stems to the notes below.

Grade 1 Music Theory Untangled Course Worksheets
© 2024 Jane Stavrinoudis. All rights reserved. Unauthorised reproduction is illegal. For more courses and piano sheet music visit the website and subscribe to the YouTube channel for Jane Stavrinoudis Piano

QUESTION 9: Add stems and beams to the quaver notes below.

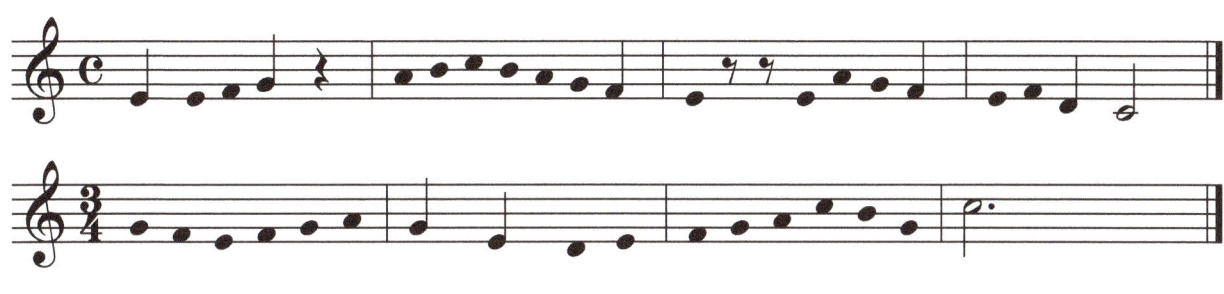

QUESTION 10: Add barlines to these melodies.

QUESTION 11: Use ticks ✓ and crosses ✗ to indicate which beams are correct or incorrect.

QUESTION 12: Complete the empty bars with any of the suggested rhythm patterns below OR create your own. Remember to check the time signature.

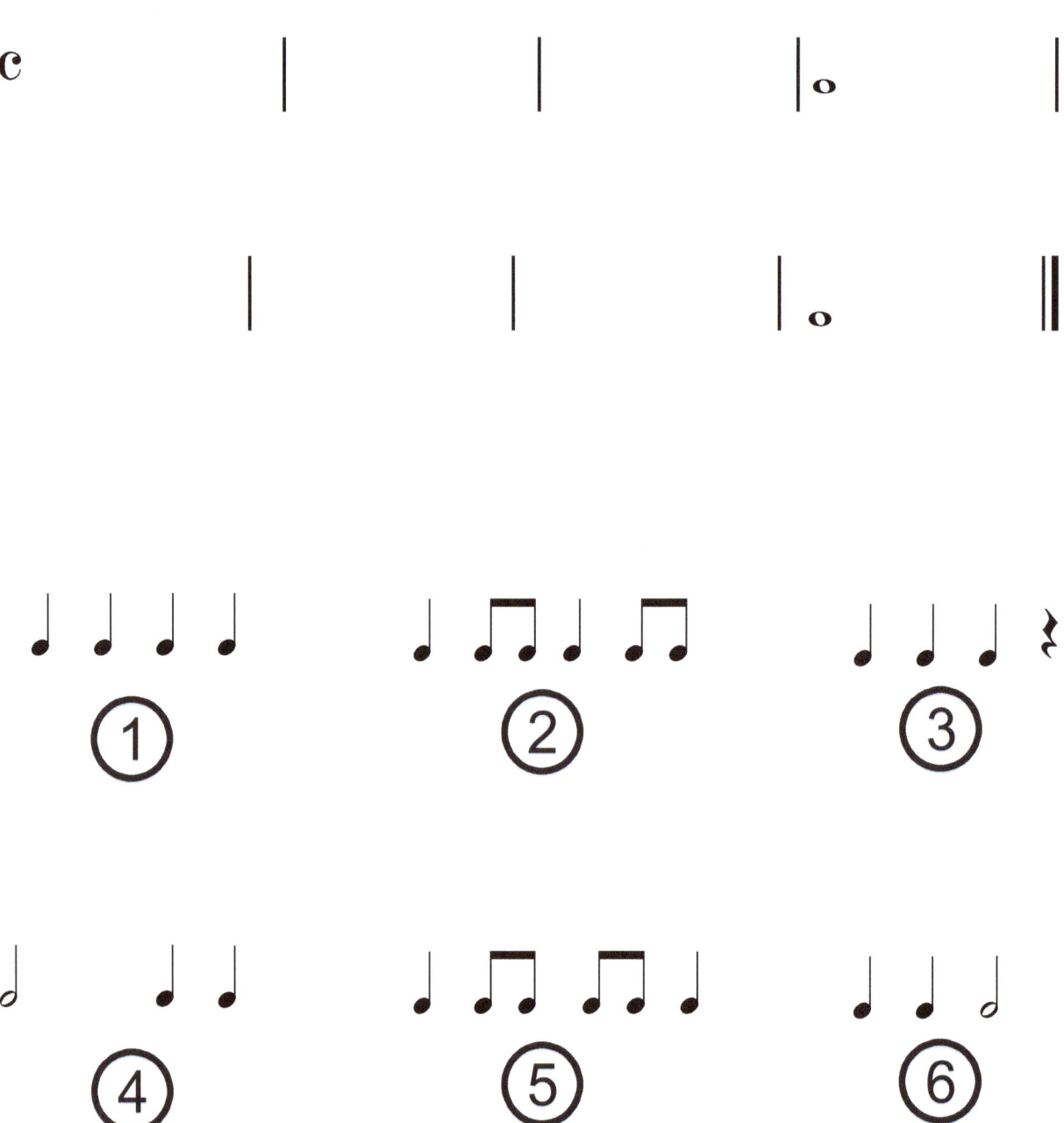

QUESTION 13: ELEMENTS OF MUSIC – LISTENING – DURATION

Click on the link and listen to the piece (or look it up on YouTube). Tick the answers that apply OVERALL while you listen. You may have to hear the piece three or four times to complete the sheet, and not all the options are used, only some!

Title: Apache	Composer: The Shadows	Link: https://www.youtube.com/watch?v=-ss22jmrs_E
DURATION: The length of time a pitch is sounded.		
What is the tempo?		
Does it change?		
If it changes, what does it change to?		
Are there many rhythmic ideas or just a few?		
How long or short are the sounds?		
Are there silences?		
How are the silences used?		
What is the effect of the silences?		
What rhythm patterns are featured?		
RHYTHM: The combinations of long, short, even or uneven sounds that convey the flow of music in time.		
METRE	Is the Time Signature: ☐ simple, ☐ compound or ☐ other	
	Does the time signature change? ☐ No ☐ Yes to _____	
	Are there any cross rhythms *(two different time signatures)*? ☐ Yes ☐ No	
	How many beats are there per bar? ☐ 2 ☐ 3 ☐ 4 ☐ 5 ☐ other	
	Are the phrases ☐ balanced *(equal in length)* or ☐ unbalanced?	
NOTE VALUES	What notes are used? ☐ ♩ ☐ ♫ ☐ ♪ ☐ 𝅗𝅥 ☐ 𝅗𝅥. ☐ 𝅝 ☐ other	
	Is there an anacrusis *(lead in or incomplete bar at the start)*? ☒ Yes ☐ No	
	Is the piece ☒ Metrical *(on the beat)*, ☐ syncopated *(on the weak beats)* or ☐ a mixture	
	Is there any Rubato *(free of the beat)*? ☐ No ☐ Yes	
	Are there any Polyrhythms *(two or more independent rhythms)*? ☐ Yes ☐ No	
	Are there any repetitive patterns? ☐ Ostinato ☐ Loop ☐ Other ☐ No	
	Is there any motivic development *(does the melody change)*? ☐ Yes ☐ No	
TEMPO *(speed)*	☐ Presto *(very fast)* ☐ Allegro *(fast)* ☐ Vivace *(fast and lively)* ☐ Allegretto *(moderately quick and cheerful)*	
	☐ Moderato *(moderately)* ☐ Andante *(at a moderate walking pace)* ☐ Adagio *(slowly)*	
	☐ Lento *(broadly, slow)* ☐ Largo *(very slow)* ☐ Grave *(slow and serious)*	
	Are there any changes in speed? ☐ No ☐ Yes: ☐ accel ☐ rall	

Grade 1 Music Theory Untangled Course Worksheets

LESSON 3 NOTE NAMES AND KEY SIGNATURES

Watch this video first:

https://youtu.be/XJ2lcbRPw1M

Work through this online quiz:

https://www.flexiquiz.com/SC/N/1c3326dc-607e-4347-bb86-2d0d1e0ffe72

QUESTION 1: Use the letters **L** and **S** to indicate whether the notes are on a line or in a space.

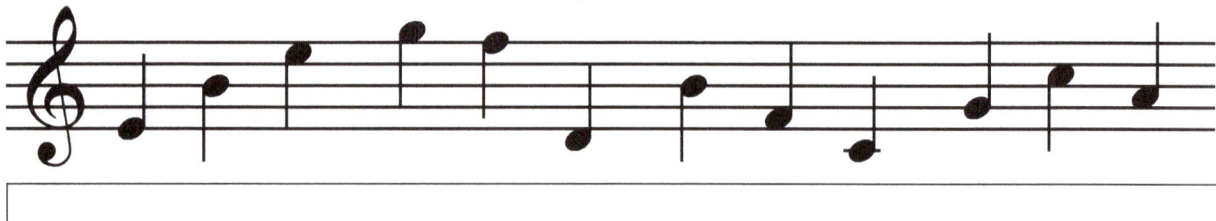

QUESTION 2: Use the letters **St** and **Sk** to indicate whether the pairs of notes are steps or skips

QUESTION 3: Name these notes.

QUESTION 4: Name these notes.

QUESTION 5: Name these notes.

QUESTION 6: Draw a line joining the stave to the correct key signature.

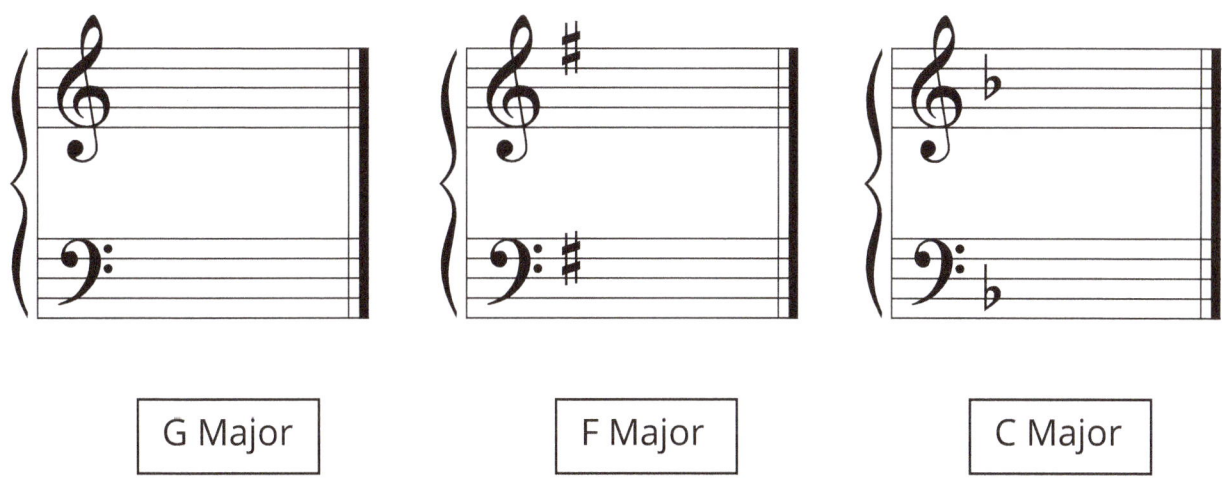

QUESTION 7: Write the key signatures on the staves below.

QUESTION 8: Complete the empty bars with any of the suggested rhythm patterns below OR create your own. Remember to check the time signature.

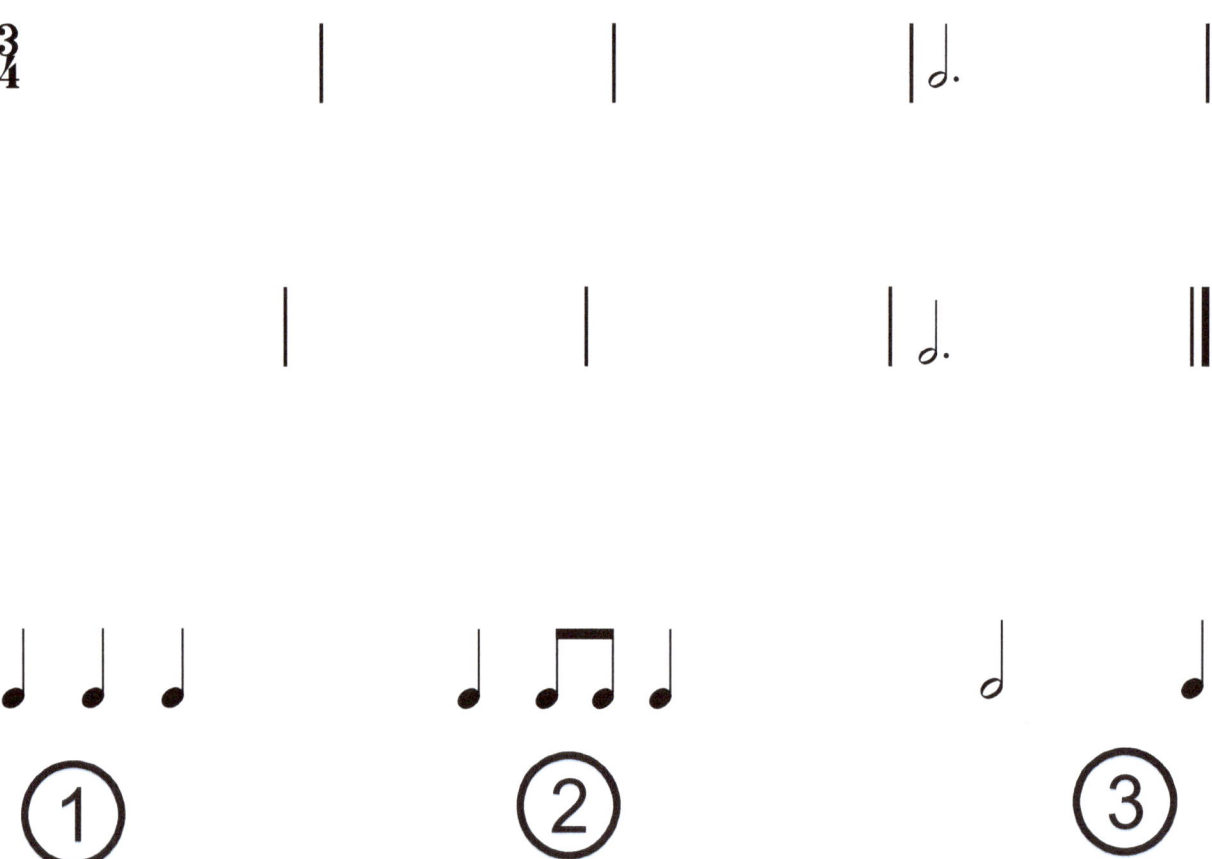

QUESTION 9: ELEMENTS OF MUSIC – LISTENING – DURATION

Click on the link and listen to the piece (or look it up on YouTube). Tick the answers that apply OVERALL while you listen. You may have to hear the piece three or four times to complete the sheet, and not all the options are used, only some!

Title: Russians	**Composer:** Sting	**Link:** https://www.youtube.com/watch?v=wHylQRVN2Qs
DURATION: The length of time a pitch is sounded.		
What is the tempo?		
Does it change?		
If it changes, what does it change to?		
Are there many rhythmic ideas or just a few?		
How long or short are the sounds?		
Are there silences?		
How are the silences used?		
What is the effect of the silences?		
What rhythm patterns are featured?		
RHYTHM: The combinations of long, short, even or uneven sounds that convey the flow of music in time.		
METRE	Is the Time Signature: ☐ simple, ☐ compound or ☐ other	
	Does the time signature change? ☐ No ☐ Yes to _____	
	Are there any cross rhythms *(two different time signatures)*? ☐ Yes ☐ No	
	How many beats are there per bar? ☐ 2 ☐ 3 ☐ 4 ☐ 5 ☐ other	
	Are the phrases ☐ balanced *(equal in length)* or ☐ unbalanced?	
NOTE VALUES	What notes are used? ☐ ♩ ☐ ♫ ☐ ♪ ☐ 𝅗𝅥 ☐ 𝅗𝅥. ☐ 𝅝 ☐ other	
	Is there an anacrusis *(lead in or incomplete bar at the start)*? ☐ Yes ☐ No	
	Is the piece ☐ Metrical *(on the beat)*, ☐ syncopated *(on the weak beats)* or ☐ a mixture	
	Is there any Rubato *(free of the beat)*? ☐ No ☐ Yes	
	Are there any Polyrhythms *(two or more independent rhythms)*? ☐ Yes ☐ No	
	Are there any repetitive patterns? ☐ Ostinato ☐ Loop ☐ Other ☐ No	
	Is there any motivic development *(does the melody change)*? ☐ Yes ☐ No	
TEMPO *(speed)*	☐ Presto *(very fast)* ☐ Allegro *(fast)* ☐ Vivace *(fast and lively)* ☐ Allegretto *(moderately quick and cheerful)*	
	☐ Moderato *(moderately)* ☐ Andante *(at a moderate walking pace)* ☐ Adagio *(slowly)*	
	☐ Lento *(broadly, slow)* ☐ Largo *(very slow)* ☐ Grave *(slow and serious)*	
	Are there any changes in speed? ☐ No ☐ Yes: ☐ accel ☐ rall	

Grade 1 Music Theory Untangled Course Worksheets

LESSON 4 TONES AND SEMITONES

Watch this video first:

https://youtu.be/EldNkWlKd5U

Work through this online quiz:

https://www.flexiquiz.com/SC/N/8d1ef05f-8b60-4437-9e63-53bc854e72bc

QUESTION 1: Label each pair of symbols as Tone or Semitone:

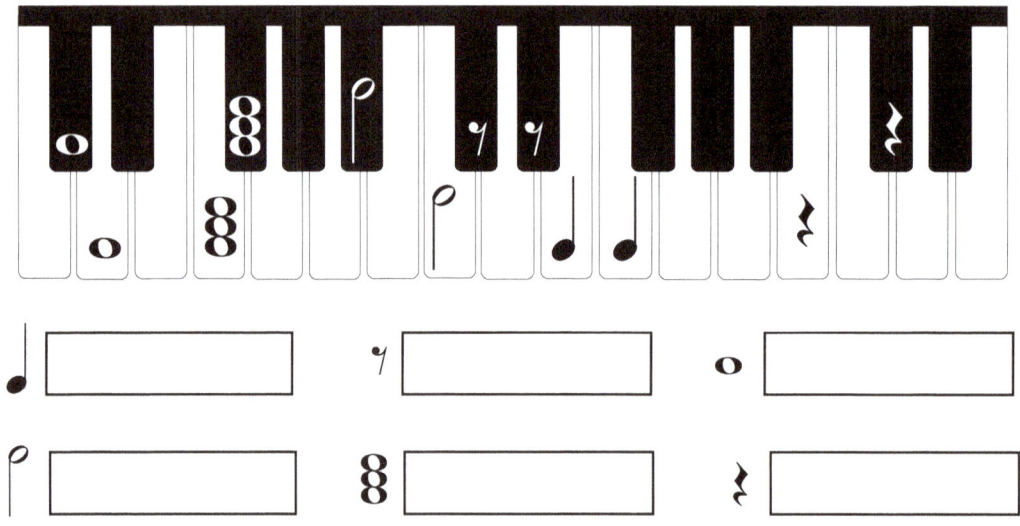

QUESTION 2: Complete each sentence.

♯ This symbol is called a _____ and it _____ the note by _____ semitone.

♭ This symbol is called a _____ and it _____ the note by _____ semitone.

♮ This symbol is called a _____ and it _____ the previous_____ and _____ .

QUESTION 3: Name these notes then label the distance between them as **T** for tone and **S** for semitone.

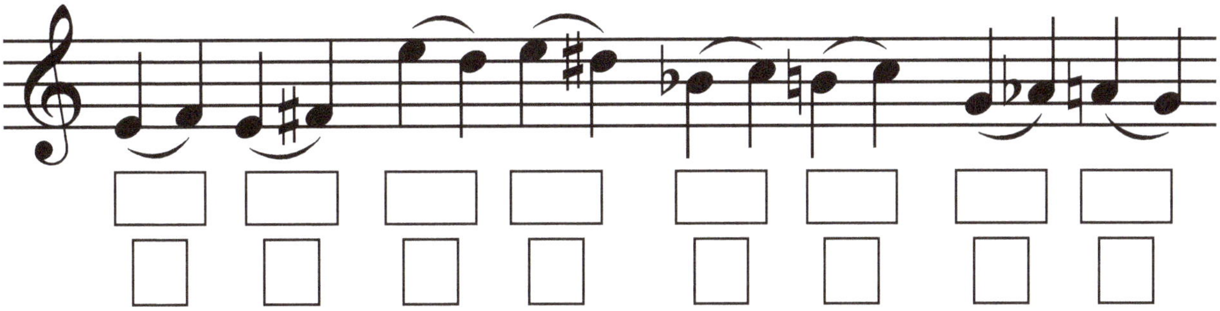

QUESTION 4: Write in the missing time signature for these melodies.

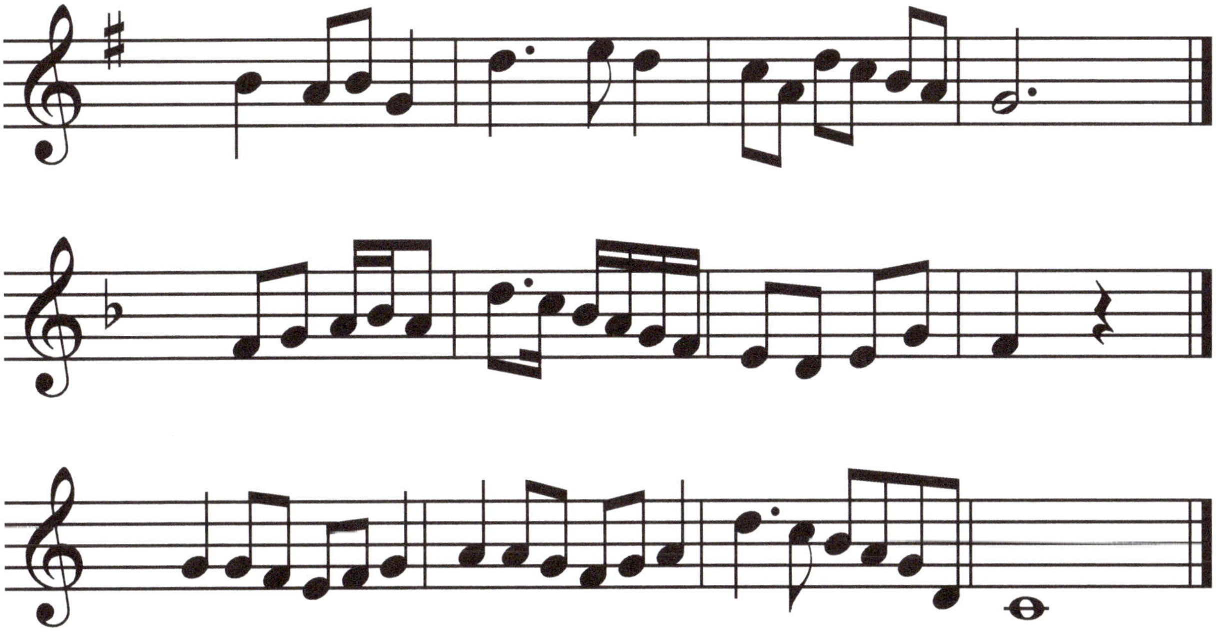

QUESTION 5: Match these notes to the correct clef. 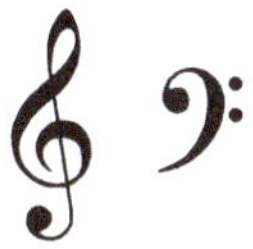

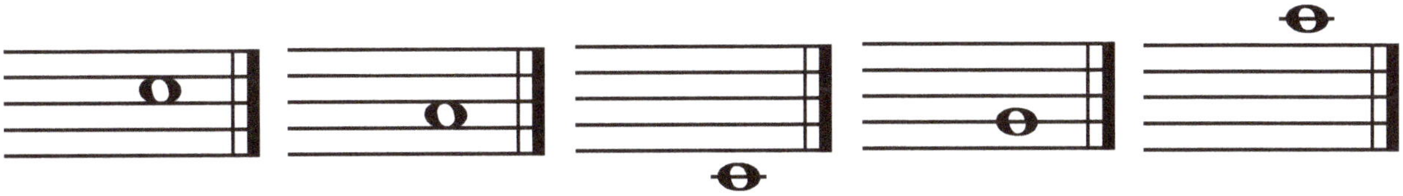

C C C G C

Grade 1 Music Theory Untangled Course Worksheets

QUESTION 6: Rewrite the rhythm pattern and add pitch to write a melody. Remember to check the key signature and move by step or small intervals.

QUESTION 7: ELEMENTS OF MUSIC – LISTENING – DURATION

Click on the link and listen to the piece (or look it up on YouTube). Tick the answers that apply OVERALL while you listen. You may have to hear the piece three or four times to complete the sheet, and not all the options are used, only some!

Title: Peter Gunn Theme	Composer: Henri Mancini	Link: https://www.youtube.com/watch?v=9DgFOsEs-kE

DURATION: The length of time a pitch is sounded.	
What is the tempo?	
Does it change?	
If it changes, what does it change to?	
Are there many rhythmic ideas or just a few?	
How long or short are the sounds?	
Are there silences?	
How are the silences used?	
What is the effect of the silences?	
What rhythm patterns are featured?	

RHYTHM: The combinations of long, short, even or uneven sounds that convey the flow of music in time.	
METRE	Is the Time Signature: ☐ simple, ☐ compound or ☐ other
	Does the time signature change? ☐ No ☐ Yes to _____
	Are there any cross rhythms *(two different time signatures)*? ☐ Yes ☐ No
	How many beats are there per bar? ☐ 2 ☐ 3 ☐ 4 ☐ 5 ☐ other
	Are the phrases ☐ balanced *(equal in length)* or ☐ unbalanced?
NOTE VALUES	What notes are used? ☐ ♩ ☐ ♫ ☐ ♪ ☐ 𝅗𝅥 ☐ 𝅗𝅥. ☐ 𝅝 ☐ other
	Is there an anacrusis *(lead in or incomplete bar at the start)*? ☐ Yes ☐ No
	Is the piece ☐ Metrical *(on the beat)*, ☐ syncopated *(on the weak beats)* or ☐ a mixture
	Is there any Rubato *(free of the beat)*? ☐ No ☐ Yes
	Are there any Polyrhythms *(two or more independent rhythms)*? ☐ Yes ☐ No
	Are there any repetitive patterns? ☐ Ostinato ☐ Loop ☐ Other ☐ No
	Is there any motivic development *(does the melody change)*? ☐ Yes ☐ No
TEMPO *(speed)*	☐ Presto *(very fast)* ☐ Allegro *(fast)* ☐ Vivace *(fast and lively)* ☐ Allegretto *(moderately quick and cheerful)*
	☐ Moderato *(moderately)* ☐ Andante *(at a moderate walking pace)* ☐ Adagio *(slowly)* ☐ Lento *(broadly, slow)*
	☐ Largo *(very slow)* ☐ Grave *(slow and serious)*
	Are there any changes in speed? ☐ No ☐ Yes: ☐ accel ☐ rall

LESSON 5 SCALES

Watch this video first:

https://youtu.be/_cftEA1n8FA

Work through this online quiz:

https://www.flexiquiz.com/SC/N/0b8026c3-6af3-46ec-ab78-8f8cd05c6317

QUESTION 1: Under each of these notes in the C major scale, write the scale degree number then circle the semitones.

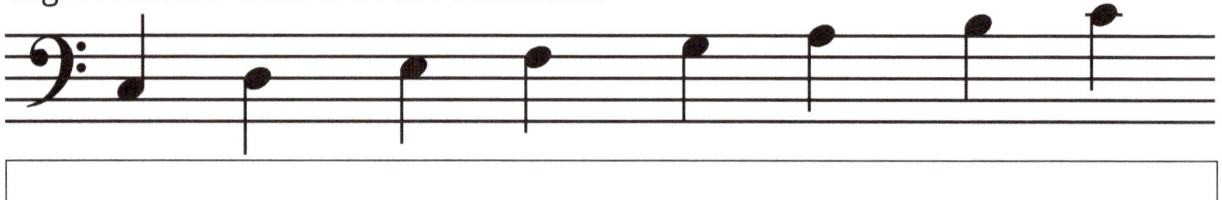

QUESTION 2: Under each of these notes in the C major scale, write the scale degree number then circle the semitones.

QUESTION 3: Under each of these notes in this melody, write the scale degree number then slur any semitones.

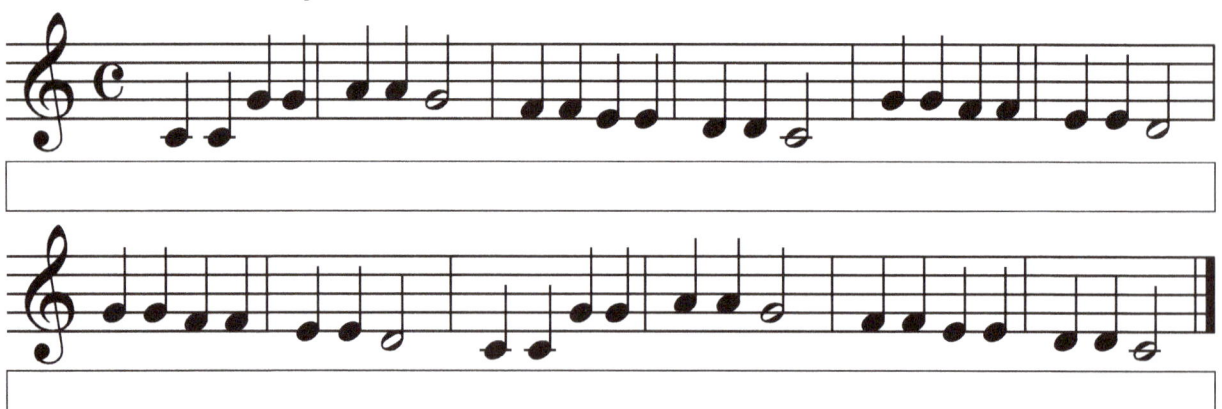

QUESTION 4: Under this scale, write the scale degree number then slur any semitones.

QUESTION 5: Add stems then write the scale degree number and circle the tones.

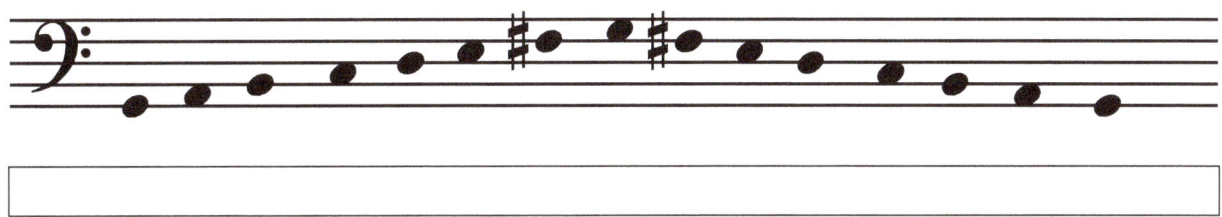

QUESTION 6 Add stems then write the scale degree number and circle the tones.

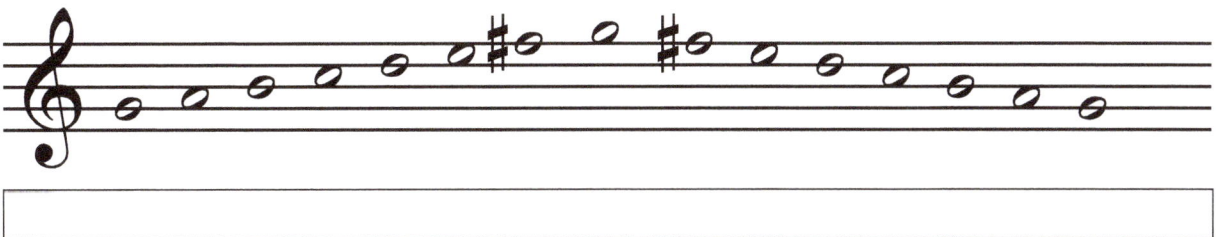

QUESTION 7: Add the stems then under this scale, write the scale degree number then slur any semitones.

QUESTION 8: Name these notes.

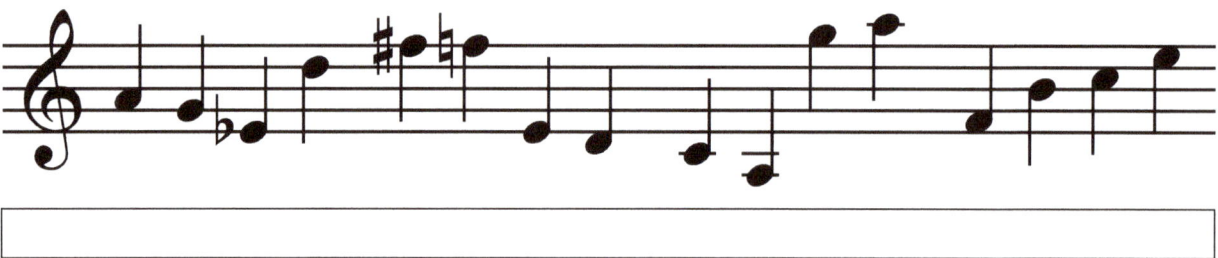

QUESTION 9: Rewrite the rhythm pattern and add pitch to write a melody. Remember to check the key signature and move by step or small intervals.

QUESTION 10: ELEMENTS OF MUSIC – LISTENING – PITCH

Click on the link and listen to the piece (or look it up on YouTube). Tick the answers that apply OVERALL while you listen. You may have to hear the piece three or four times to complete the sheet, and not all the options are used, only some!

Title Those Were The Days	Composer Boris Fomin	Link https://www.youtube.com/watch?v=ozCoq4osSwk

What is the pitch of the melody?	
What is the melodic contour (shape) of the melody?	
Does the melody move by steps or leaps, does it move up or down?	
Is the overall tonality major, minor, modal? Is there a change of key?	

MELODY: An organised sequence of single notes.

TONALITY	What scale is used? ☐ Major ☐ Minor ☐ Blues ☐ Other: _____
STRUCTURE	How many bars in each phrase? ☐ 2 ☐ 4 ☐ 8 ☐ other _____
	Are the phrases ☐ arched ☐ spiky or ☐ a mixture?
	Are the cadences *(endings)* ☐ predictable or ☐ unpredictable?
	Does the melody move by ☐ step *(conjunct)*
	☐ skip *(broken chord based)* ☐ leap *(disjunct)* ☐ chromatically or ☐ a mixture
	If a song, is it ☐ strophic *(verse/chorus)* or ☐ through-composed?
	Is there any ☐ repetition or ☐ imitation?
STYLE	Does the melody have ☐ vocal *(easy to sing)* or ☐ instrumental origins?
	What is the style? ☐ Jazz ☐ Rock ☐ Movie ☐ Folk ☐ Other

HARMONY: The simultaneous sound of two or more notes.

TONALITY	Are the chords ☐ major, ☐ minor or ☐ a mixture
CHORD PROGRESSIONS	Are the chords ☐ dissonant *(clash)* or ☐ consonant *(they fit)*?
	Is there a ☐ 12 bar Blues, ☐ 16 bar pattern or ☐ other?
	Are the cadences *(endings)* ☐ perfect *(V-I)*
	☐ imperfect *(I-V)* ☐ plagal *(IV-I)* or ☐ interrupted *(V-vi)* ?
	Is the Harmonic Rhythm *(rate of chord changes)* ☐ fast ☐ medium ☐ slow?
	Are there any modulations *(key changes)*? ☐ No ☐ Yes
	What is the relationship between the old and new keys? _____
	Is there a: ☐ Tierce de Picardie *(a major 3rd in the final chord of a minor key)*
	☐ drone *(sustained part - tonic and dominant)* ☐ suspension ☐ ornaments

LESSON 6 INTERVALS

Watch this video first:

https://youtu.be/54O_oVC2Hcw

Work through this online quiz:

https://www.flexiquiz.com/SC/N/d5064e13-0118-41d7-bfb6-f3b74972a5ff

QUESTION 1: Name these intervals.

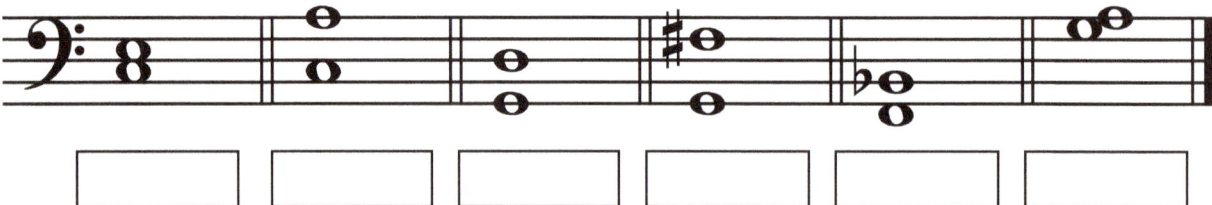

☐ ☐ ☐ ☐ ☐ ☐

QUESTION 2: Write scale degree 1 as a semibreve in each key, then the interval above.

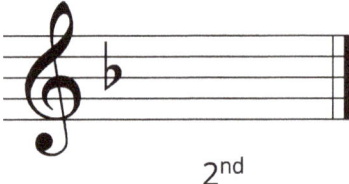      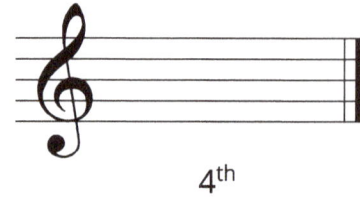

     2nd 7th 4th

QUESTION 3: Write scale degree 1 as a semibreve in each key, then the interval above.

   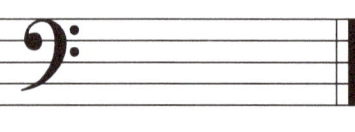   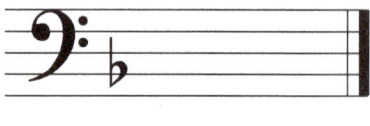

     3rd 7th 5th

QUESTION 4: Add a clef and key signature to make this scale in F major, mark the semitones with slurs, then circle the 5th scale degree.

QUESTION 5: Add a clef and key signature to make this scale in G major, mark the semitones with slurs, then circle the 4th scale degree.

QUESTION 6:
Label the interval at each slur in the melody below as 2nd, 3rd, 4th, 5th or 6th.

QUESTION 7:
Label the interval at each slur in the melody below as 2nd, 3rd, 4th, 5th or 6th.

QUESTION 8:
Label the interval at each slur in the melody below as 2nd, 3rd, 4th, 5th or 6th.

QUESTION 9: Rewrite the rhythm pattern and add pitch to write a melody. Remember to check the key signature and move by step or small intervals.

QUESTION 10: ELEMENTS OF MUSIC – LISTENING – PITCH

Click on the link and listen to the piece (or look it up on YouTube). Tick the answers that apply OVERALL while you listen. You may have to hear the piece three or four times to complete the sheet, and not all the options are used, only some!

Title 'La Réjouissance' from Fireworks Suite	Composer George Frideric Handel	Link https://www.youtube.com/watch?v=p5jgSVw3nms
What is the pitch of the melody?		
What is the melodic contour (shape) of the melody?		
Does the melody move by steps or leaps, does it move up or down?		
Is the overall tonality major, minor, modal? Is there a change of key?		
MELODY: An organised sequence of single notes.		
TONALITY	What scale is used? ☐ Major ☐ Minor ☐ Blues ☐ Other: _____	
STRUCTURE	How many bars in each phrase? ☐ 2 ☐ 4 ☐ 8 ☐ other _____	
	Are the phrases ☐ arched ☐ spiky or ☐ a mixture?	
	Are the cadences *(endings)* ☐ predictable or ☐ unpredictable?	
	Does the melody move by ☐ step *(conjunct)*	
	☐ skip *(broken chord based)* ☐ leap *(disjunct)* ☐ chromatically or ☐ a mixture	
	If a song, is it ☐ strophic *(verse/chorus)* or ☐ through-composed?	
	Is there any ☐ repetition or ☐ imitation?	
STYLE	Does the melody have ☐ vocal *(easy to sing)* or ☒ instrumental origins?	
	What is the style? ☐ Jazz ☐ Rock ☐ Movie ☐ Folk ☒ Other	
HARMONY: The simultaneous sound of two or more notes.		
TONALITY	Are the chords ☐ major, ☐ minor or ☐ a mixture	
CHORD PROGRESSIONS	Are the chords ☐ dissonant *(clash)* or ☐ consonant *(they fit)*?	
	Is there a ☐ 12 bar Blues, ☐ 16 bar pattern or ☐ other?	
	Are the cadences *(endings)* ☐ perfect *(V-I)*	
	☐ imperfect *(I-V)* ☐ plagal *(IV-I)* or ☐ interrupted *(V-vi)* ?	
	Is the Harmonic Rhythm *(rate of chord changes)* ☐ fast ☐ medium ☐ slow?	
	Are there any modulations *(key changes)*? ☐ No ☐ Yes	
	What is the relationship between the old and new keys? _____	
	Is there a: ☐ Tierce de Picardie *(a major 3rd in the final chord of a minor key)*	
	☐ drone *(sustained part - tonic and dominant)* ☐ suspension ☐ ornaments	

LESSON 7 TRIADS

Watch this video first:

https://youtu.be/A8FG5ycXHhY

Work through this online quiz:

https://www.flexiquiz.com/SC/N/ebfb1f29-7149-487a-b75d-a3f31eb90938

QUESTION 1: Complete the tonic triads below:

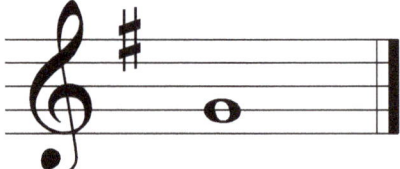  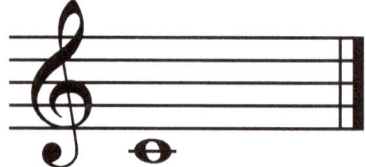

QUESTION 2: Write the tonic triad using semibreves in the major keys below:

 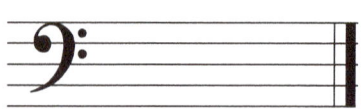 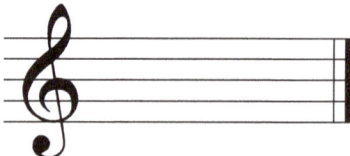

QUESTION 3: Write the tonic triad using minims in the major keys below without a key signature:

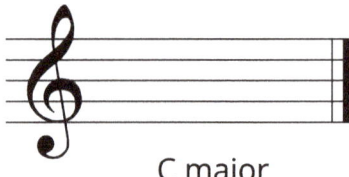  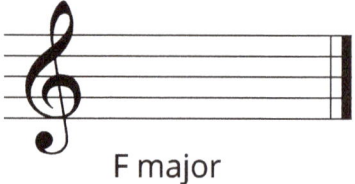

C major   G major   F major

QUESTION 4: Write the key signature then the tonic triad using crotchets:

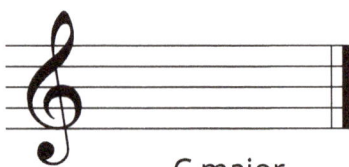  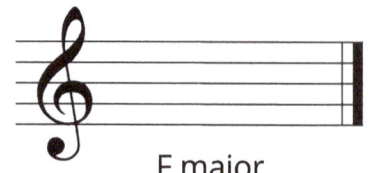

C major   G major   F major

QUESTION 5:
Draw a line joining the triad to the correct key signature.

QUESTION 6:
Write the missing note to complete each triad.

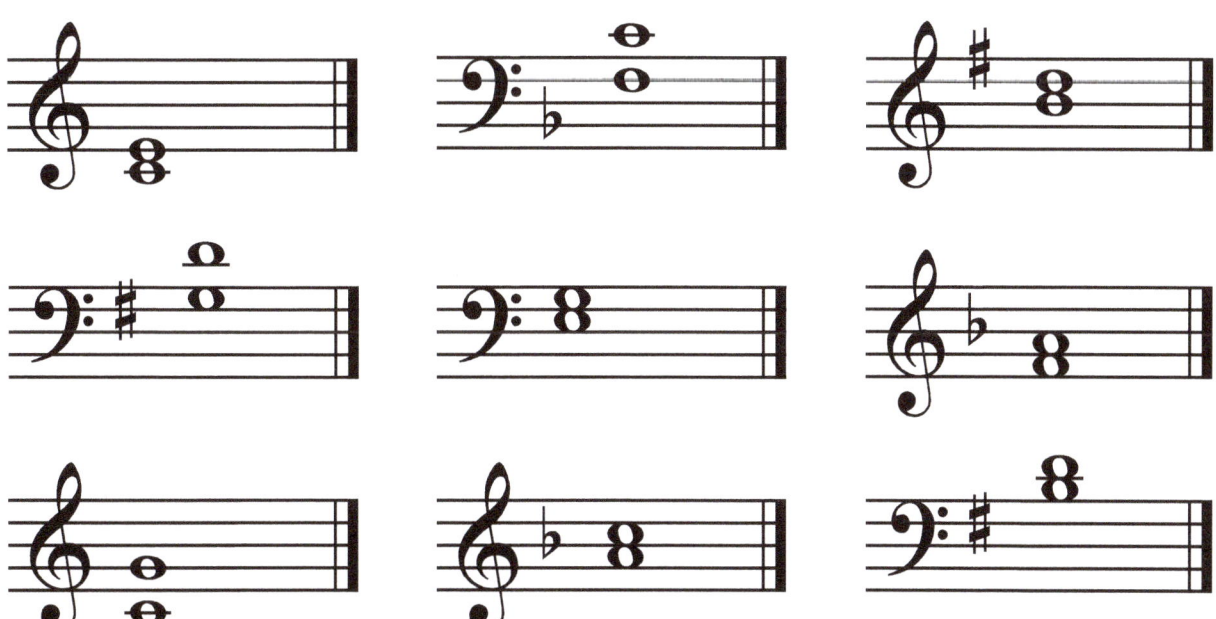

QUESTION 7: ELEMENTS OF MUSIC – LISTENING – PITCH

Click on the link and listen to the piece (or look it up on YouTube). Tick the answers that apply OVERALL while you listen. You may have to hear the piece three or four times to complete the sheet, and not all the options are used, only some!

Title Altal Mennek	Composer Magyar Roza	Link https://www.youtube.com/watch?v=fDd8w67MPWs
	What is the pitch of the melody?	
	What is the melodic contour (shape) of the melody?	
	Does the melody move by steps or leaps, does it move up or down?	
	Is the overall tonality major, minor, modal? Is there a change of key?	
MELODY: An organised sequence of single notes.		
TONALITY	What scale is used? ☐ Major ☐ Minor ☐ Blues ☐ Other	
STRUCTURE	How many bars in each phrase? ☐ 2 ☐ 4 ☐ 8 ☐ other	
	Are the phrases ☐ arched ☐ spiky or ☐ a mixture?	
	Are the cadences *(endings)* ☐ predictable or ☐ unpredictable?	
	Does the melody move by ☐ step *(conjunct)*	
	☐ skip *(broken chord based)* ☐ leap *(disjunct)* ☐ chromatically or ☐ a mixture	
	If a song, is it ☐ strophic *(verse/chorus)* or ☐ through-composed?	
	Is there any ☐ repetition or ☐ imitation?	
STYLE	Does the melody have ☐ vocal *(easy to sing)* or ☐ instrumental origins?	
	What is the style? ☐ Jazz ☐ Rock ☐ Movie ☐ Folk ☐ Other	
HARMONY: The simultaneous sound of two or more notes.		
TONALITY	Are the chords ☐ major, ☐ minor or ☐ a mixture	
CHORD PROGRESSIONS	Are the chords ☐ dissonant *(clash)* or ☐ consonant *(they fit)*?	
	Is there a ☐ 12 bar Blues, ☐ 16 bar pattern or ☐ other?	
	Are the cadences *(endings)* ☐ perfect *(V-I)*	
	☐ imperfect *(I-V)* ☐ plagal *(IV-I)* or ☐ interrupted *(V-vi)* ?	
	Is the Harmonic Rhythm *(rate of chord changes)* ☐ fast ☐ medium ☐ slow?	
	Are there any modulations *(key changes)*? ☐ No ☐ Yes	
	What is the relationship between the old and new keys? _____	
	Is there a: ☐ Tierce de Picardie *(a major 3rd in the final chord of a minor key)*	
	☐ drone *(sustained part - tonic and dominant)* ☐ suspension ☐ ornaments	

LESSON 8 TRANSPOSITION

Watch this video first:

https://youtu.be/qDfU_yj1YIA

Work through this online quiz:

https://www.flexiquiz.com/SC/N/b5d8626e-e5ce-4271-98e4-cd2a6cd95cbc

QUESTION 1: Transpose this melody up one octave.

QUESTION 2: Transpose this melody up into C Major.

Grade 1 Music Theory Untangled Course Worksheets
© 2024 Jane Stavrinoudis. All rights reserved. Unauthorised reproduction is illegal. For more courses and piano sheet music visit the website and subscribe to the YouTube channel for Jane Stavrinoudis Piano

QUESTION 3: Transpose this melody down one octave.

QUESTION 4: Transpose this melody down into G Major.

QUESTION 5: Transpose this melody up into F Major.

QUESTION 6: Rewrite this melody from treble to bass clef.

QUESTION 7: Write the term for each definition below, then find that word in the puzzle.

	Gradually becoming faster
	The note is to be louder, with more attack
	Slowly
	Music is divided by bar lines into these
	Symbol for low sounds
	Lyrically, in a singing style
	Gradually becoming softer
	Pause; lengthen the value of the note or rest
	An interval of seven semitones between two notes
	The end of the piece
	Lowers a note by one semitone
	Very loud
	The major or minor scale around which a piece of music revolves
	A half note
	Cancels a previous sharp or flat
	The difference in pitch between the first and last notes in a music scale
	A work or group of works
	Very softly
	Four
	Gradually becoming slower
	Silence
	A whole note
	The distance between one note and the very next

Grade 1 Music Theory Untangled Course Worksheets

U	C	W	A	R	Z	D	N	U	N	V	E	Q	R	E	G
O	A	S	F	T	A	Q	I	T	B	A	S	S	U	D	F
C	N	X	B	O	V	L	S	M	Y	M	T	V	P	I	H
E	T	R	O	U	R	D	L	R	I	O	F	U	O	C	B
P	A	Y	V	D	Z	T	Q	E	P	N	W	T	R	J	L
N	B	Q	A	W	N	K	I	W	N	G	U	X	N	A	K
F	I	F	T	H	Y	E	P	S	H	T	H	E	Y	M	L
M	L	Z	B	X	I	G	R	X	S	F	A	S	N	A	A
F	E	R	M	A	T	A	O	E	E	I	L	N	Y	D	Z
L	W	K	C	J	D	C	N	Y	L	D	M	Z	D	B	O
S	E	M	I	T	O	N	E	Z	C	E	Y	O	R	O	C
E	T	E	I	K	B	H	M	R	A	X	C	Q	X	E	G
M	Q	G	D	J	K	G	L	Q	E	W	N	C	U	D	F
I	U	F	H	S	P	F	P	W	B	S	U	I	A	H	E
B	A	C	C	E	N	T	V	X	J	V	T	B	W	V	J
R	D	I	O	R	E	U	F	M	T	A	S	O	A	I	L
E	R	N	J	M	D	A	H	J	L	G	L	T	D	R	K
V	U	L	M	I	T	S	R	F	Q	S	C	P	A	S	M
E	P	I	A	N	I	S	S	I	M	O	U	N	G	T	R
A	L	B	C	I	C	E	G	N	I	K	M	P	I	P	N
K	E	Y	A	M	B	D	F	E	H	J	L	P	O	Q	O

Grade 1 Music Theory Untangled Course Worksheets
© 2024 Jane Stavrinoudis. All rights reserved. Unauthorised reproduction is illegal. For more courses and piano sheet music visit the website and subscribe to the YouTube channel for Jane Stavrinoudis Piano

LESSON 9 TERMS AND DEFINITIONS

Watch this video first:

https://youtu.be/DDy_C5_-4zs

Work through this online quiz:

https://www.flexiquiz.com/SC/N/6b50d5d5-49f9-4e32-8cc5-db7f2fd55a79

1. What is the English meaning of *Allegro*?

2. What is the meaning of the sign under the first note?

3. How many quavers are to be played staccato?

4. What is the full name of the term above the last two notes in bar 3?

5. How many slurs does this melody contain?

6. Does this melody contain a tie?

7. Does this melody contain a crescendo?

8. What is the meaning of the sign under the last note?

9. How should the quavers in bar 2 be played?

10. What is the English meaning of the term above bar 3?

QUESTION 11:
Write the term for each definition below, then complete the crossword puzzle.

ACROSS

2		Music is divided by bar lines into these
7		Three notes played at the same time
9		Order of Treble Clef spaces
10		Smoothly
12		Short and detached
15		A section of music added at the end
16		In a singing style
21		A whole note
22		Play again
23		With attack
24		Loud
26		Pause
28		Cancels a sharp or flat
30		The end of a piece
31		Held
33		Extra lines to extend the staff
34		Moves a note up a semitone

DOWN

1		Very fast
3		Symbol for silence
4		Slowly
5		Another name for Simple Quadruple
6		Symbol for low sounds
8		Volumes of music
11		Soft
13		Get louder
14		Lively and fast
17		Get faster
18		Moves a note down a semitone
19		Slower
20		Moderately
23		Order of Bass Clef spaces
25		Lines and spaces on which music is written
27		The tune
29		Symbol for high sounds
32		The speed of music

Music Theory
UNTANGLED COURSE
ANSWERS

GRADE 1
SECOND EDITION

BY JANE STAVRINOUDIS

Lesson 1

QUESTION 1: Simple Duple Time (2 crotchet beats per bar)

QUESTION 2: Simple Triple Time (3 crotchet beats per bar)

QUESTION 3: Simple Quadruple Time (4 crotchet beats per bar)

QUESTION 4: Common Time (Simple Quadruple Time)

QUESTION 5:

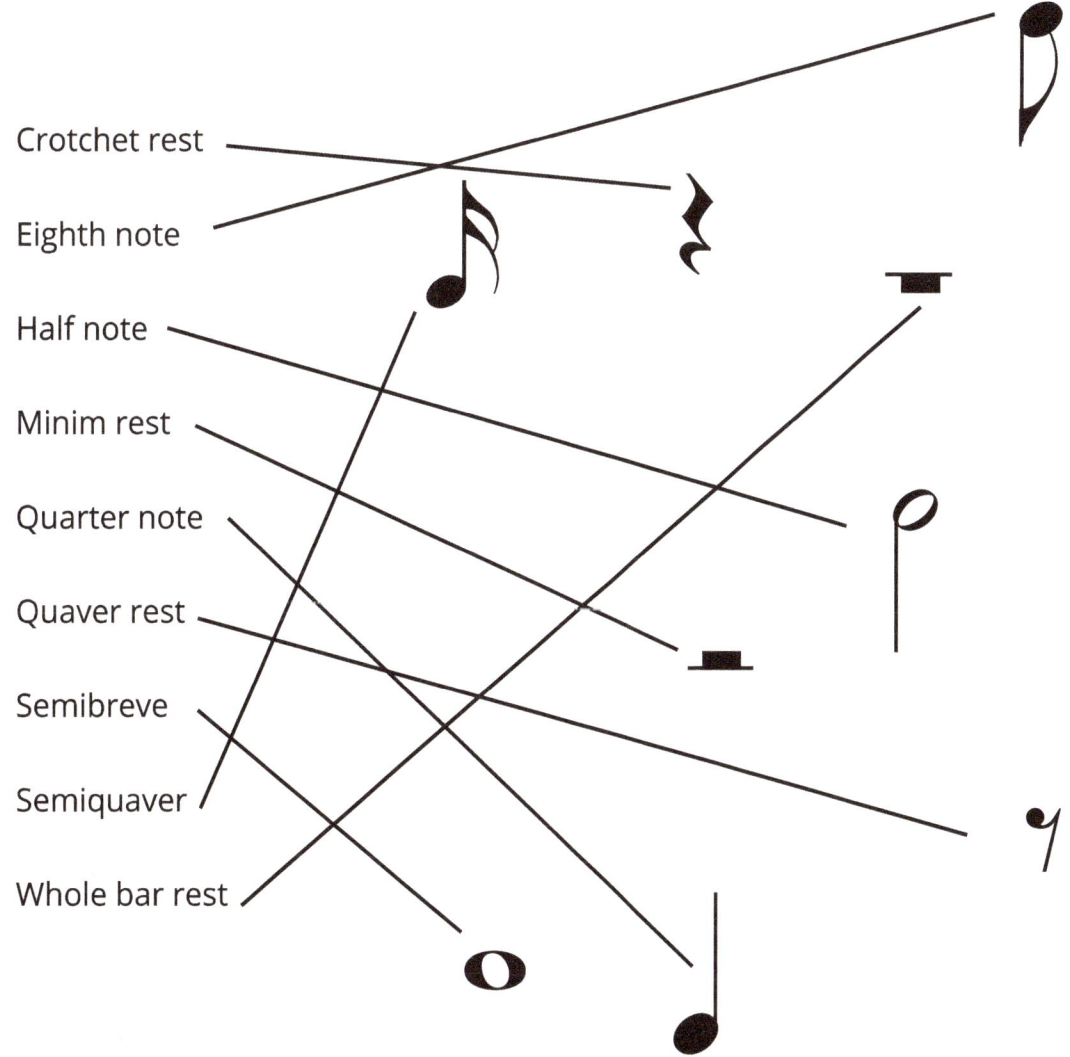

QUESTION 6:

QUESTION 7:

QUESTION 8:

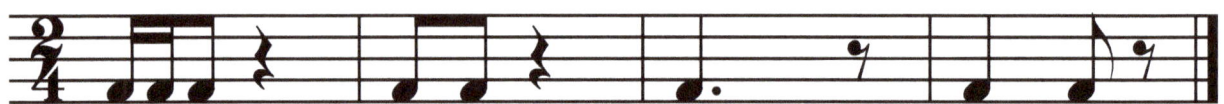

QUESTION 9:
a) Simple Quadruple
b) Simple Triple
c) Simple Duple
d) Simple Triple
e) Simple Duple
f) Simple Quadruple

Lesson 2

QUESTION 1: Treble Clef or G Clef and it notates High Sounds

QUESTION 2: Bass Clef or F Clef and it notates low sounds

QUESTION 3: Semibreve or whole note and it is 4 counts long.

QUESTION 4: Crotchet or quarter note and it is 1 count long.

QUESTION 5: Semibreve rest or whole bar rest and it is a rest for a whole bar in any time signature.

QUESTION 6: Sharp and it means raise the note by one semitone.

QUESTION 7: Natural and it means cancel the previous sharp or flat.

QUESTION 8:

QUESTION 9:

QUESTION 10:

QUESTION 11:

Grade 1 Music Theory Untangled Course Answers
© 2024 Jane Stavrinoudis. All rights reserved. Unauthorised reproduction is illegal. For more courses and piano sheet music visit the website and subscribe to the YouTube channel for Jane Stavrinoudis Piano

QUESTION 12:

Sample Answer

Sample Answer

Sample Answer

QUESTION 13:

Title: Apache	Composer: The Shadows	Link: https://www.youtube.com/watch?v=-ss22jmrs_E

DURATION: The length of time a pitch is sounded.	
What is the tempo?	**Moderate**
Does it change?	**No**
If it changes, what does it change to?	**N/A**
Are there many rhythmic ideas or just a few?	**Just a few**
How long or short are the sounds?	**Mainly short**
Are there silences?	**No**
How are the silences used?	**N/A**
What is the effect of the silences?	**N/A**
What rhythm patterns are featured?	**Simple, short, on the beat**

RHYTHM: The combinations of long, short, even or uneven sounds that convey the flow of music in time.	
METRE	Is the Time Signature: ☑ **simple**, ☐ compound or ☐ other
	Does the time signature change? ☑ **No** ☐ Yes to _____
	Are there any cross rhythms *(two different time signatures)*? ☐ Yes ☑ **No**
	How many beats are there per bar? ☐ 2 ☐ 3 ☑ **4** ☐ 5 ☐ other
	Are the phrases ☑ **balanced** *(equal in length)* or ☐ unbalanced?
NOTE VALUES	What notes are used? ☑ ♩ ☑ ♫ ☑ 𝅗𝅥 ☑ 𝅗𝅥. ☑ 𝅝 ☐ other
	Is there an anacrusis *(lead in or incomplete bar at the start)*? ☑ **Yes** ☐ No
	Is the piece ☑ **Metrical** *(on the beat)*, ☐ syncopated *(on the weak beats)* or ☐ a mixture
	Is there any Rubato *(free of the beat)*? ☑ **No** ☐ Yes
	Are there any Polyrhythms *(two or more independent rhythms)*? ☐ Yes ☑ **No**
	Are there any repetitive patterns? ☐ Ostinato ☐ Loop ☐ Other ☑ **No**
	Is there any motivic development *(does the melody change)*? ☐ Yes ☑ **No**
TEMPO *(speed)*	☐ Presto *(very fast)* ☐ Allegro *(fast)* ☐ Vivace *(fast and lively)*
	☐ Allegretto *(moderately quick and cheerful)* ☑ **Moderato** *(moderately)*
	☐ Andante *(at a moderate walking pace)* ☐ Adagio *(slowly)* ☐ Lento *(broadly, slow)*
	☐ Largo *(very slow)* ☐ Grave *(slow and serious)*
	Are there any changes in speed? ☑ **No** ☐ Yes: ☐ accel ☐ rall

Lesson 3

QUESTION 1:

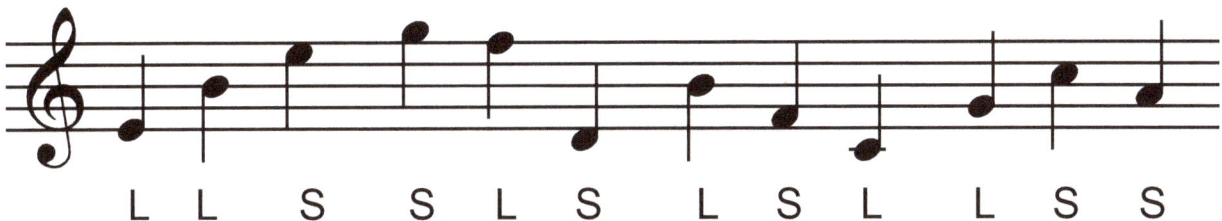

L L S S L S L S L L S S

QUESTION 2:

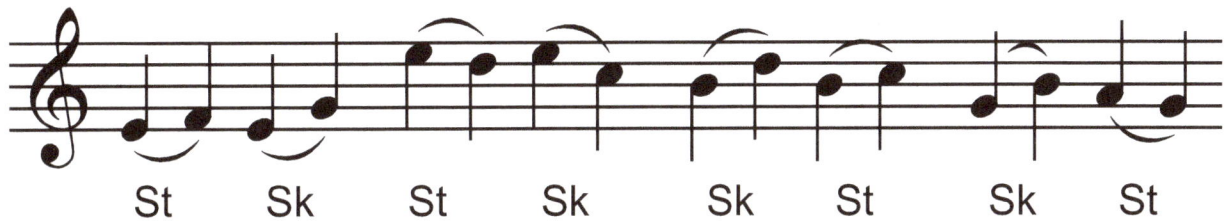

St Sk St Sk Sk St Sk St

QUESTION 3:

Bass: F E C flat B D sharp D natural C B A F E F D G A C

QUESTION 4:

Treble: E D G flat B flat C B natural F sharp A B D C B A F G C

QUESTION 5:

Bass: G sharp B G natural G flat F E B sharp D E F F E D flat B C C

QUESTION 6:

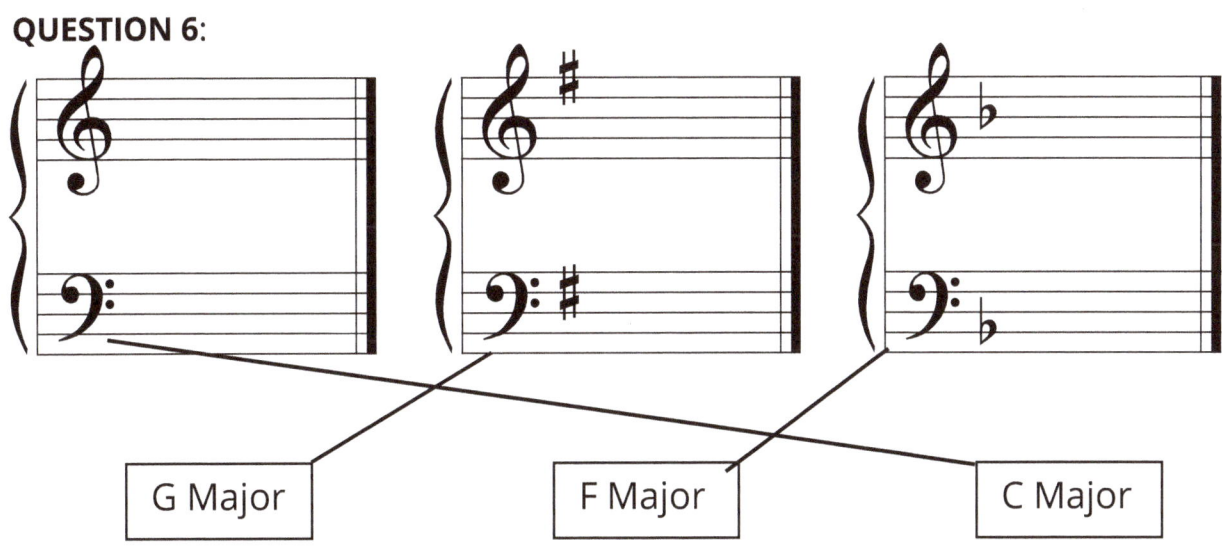

G Major   F Major   C Major

QUESTION 7:

C Major   G Major   F Major

QUESTION 8:

Sample Answer

Sample Answer

Sample Answer

QUESTION 9:

Title: Russians	Composer: Sting	Link: https://www.youtube.com/watch?v=wHylQRVN2Qs
DURATION: The length of time a pitch is sounded.		
What is the tempo?		Slow
Does it change?		No
If it changes, what does it change to?		N/A
Are there many rhythmic ideas or just a few?		Just a few
How long or short are the sounds?		Long
Are there silences?		No
How are the silences used?		N/A
What is the effect of the silences?		N/A
What rhythm patterns are featured?		On the beat, steady, long
RHYTHM: The combinations of long, short, even or uneven sounds that convey the flow of music in time.		
METRE	Is the Time Signature: ☑ **simple,** ☐ compound or ☐ other	
	Does the time signature change? ☑ **No** ☐ Yes to _____	
	Are there any cross rhythms *(two different time signatures)*? ☐ Yes ☑ **No**	
	How many beats are there per bar? ☑ **2** ☐ 3 ☐ 4 ☐ 5 ☐ other	
	Are the phrases ☑ **balanced** *(equal in length)* or ☐ unbalanced?	
NOTE VALUES	What notes are used? ☑ ♩ ☑ ♫ ☑ 𝅗𝅥 ☑ 𝅗𝅥. ☑ 𝅝 ☐ other	
	Is there an anacrusis *(lead in or incomplete bar at the start)*? ☑ **Yes** ☐ No	
	Is the piece ☑ **Metrical** *(on the beat)*, ☐ syncopated *(on the weak beats)* or ☐ a mixture	
	Is there any Rubato *(free of the beat)*? ☑ **No** ☐ Yes	
	Are there any Polyrhythms *(two or more independent rhythms)*? ☐ Yes ☑ **No**	
	Are there any repetitive patterns? ☑ **Ostinato** ☐ Loop ☐ Other ☐ No	
	Is there any motivic development *(does the melody change)*? ☐ Yes ☑ **No**	
TEMPO *(speed)*	☐ Presto *(very fast)* ☐ Allegro *(fast)* ☐ Vivace *(fast and lively)*	
	☐ Allegretto *(moderately quick and cheerful)* ☐ Moderato *(moderately)*	
	☑ **Andante *(at a moderate walking pace)*** ☐ Adagio *(slowly)* ☐ Lento *(broadly, slow)*	
	☐ Largo *(very slow)* ☐ Grave *(slow and serious)*	
	Are there any changes in speed? ☑ **No** ☐ Yes: ☐ accel ☐ rall	

Lesson 4

QUESTION 1:

QUESTION 2:

This symbol is called a sharp and raises the note by one semitone.

This symbol is called a flat and lowers the note by one semitone.

This symbol is called a natural and cancels the previous sharp or flat.

QUESTION 3:

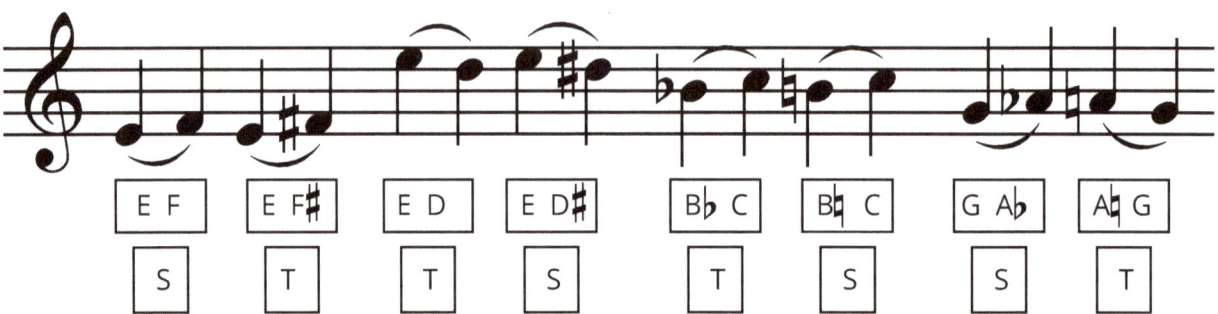

QUESTION 4:

QUESTION 5:

C   C   C   G   C

QUESTION 6:

Sample Answer

QUESTION 7:

Title: Peter Gunn Theme	Composer: Henri Mancini	Link: https://www.youtube.com/watch?v=9DgFOsEs-kE

DURATION: The length of time a pitch is sounded.	
What is the tempo?	Moderate
Does it change?	No
If it changes, what does it change to?	N/A
Are there many rhythmic ideas or just a few?	Just a few
How long or short are the sounds?	**Combination of long and short**
Are there silences?	No
How are the silences used?	N/A
What is the effect of the silences?	N/A
What rhythm patterns are featured?	**Steady, repetitive, short and long**

RHYTHM: The combinations of long, short, even or uneven sounds that convey the flow of music in time.

METRE	Is the Time Signature: ☑ **simple,** ☐ compound or ☐ other
	Does the time signature change? ☑ **No** ☐ Yes to _____
	Are there any cross rhythms *(two different time signatures)*? ☐ Yes ☑ **No**
	How many beats are there per bar? ☐ 2 ☐ 3 ☑ **4** ☐ 5 ☐ other
	Are the phrases ☑ **balanced** *(equal in length)* or ☐ unbalanced?

NOTE VALUES	What notes are used? ☑ ♩ ☑ ♫ ☑ 𝅗𝅥 ☑ 𝅗𝅥. ☑ 𝅝 ☐ other
	Is there an anacrusis *(lead in or incomplete bar at the start)*? ☐ Yes ☑ **No**
	Is the piece ☐ Metrical *(on the beat)*, ☐ syncopated *(on the weak beats)* or ☑ **a mixture**
	Is there any Rubato *(free of the beat)*? ☑ **No** ☐ Yes
	Are there any Polyrhythms *(two or more independent rhythms)*? ☐ Yes ☑ **No**
	Are there any repetitive patterns? ☑ **Ostinato** ☐ Loop ☐ Other ☐ No
	Is there any motivic development *(does the melody change)*? ☐ Yes ☑ **No**

TEMPO *(speed)*	☐ Presto *(very fast)* ☐ Allegro *(fast)* ☐ Vivace *(fast and lively)*
	☐ Allegretto *(moderately quick and cheerful)* ☑ **Moderato** *(moderately)*
	☐ Andante *(at a moderate walking pace)* ☐ Adagio *(slowly)* ☐ Lento *(broadly, slow)* ☐ Largo *(very slow)*
	☐ Grave *(slow and serious)* Are there any changes in speed? ☑ **No** ☐ Yes: ☐ accel ☐ rall

Lesson 5

QUESTION 1:

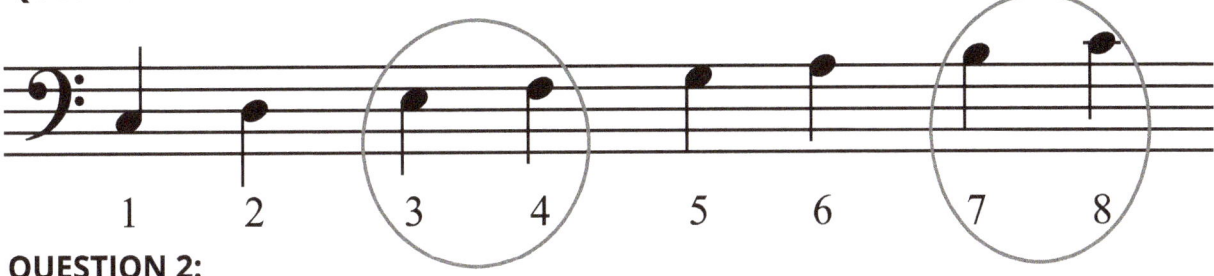

QUESTION 2:

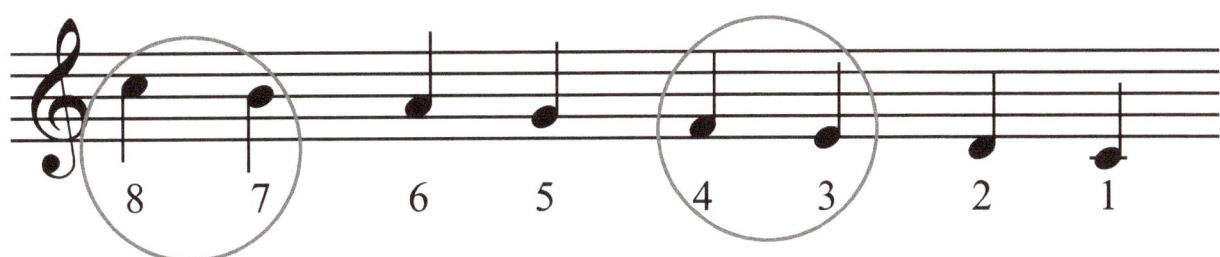

QUESTION 3: Under each of the notes in this melody, write the scale degree number then slur any semitones.

QUESTION 4:

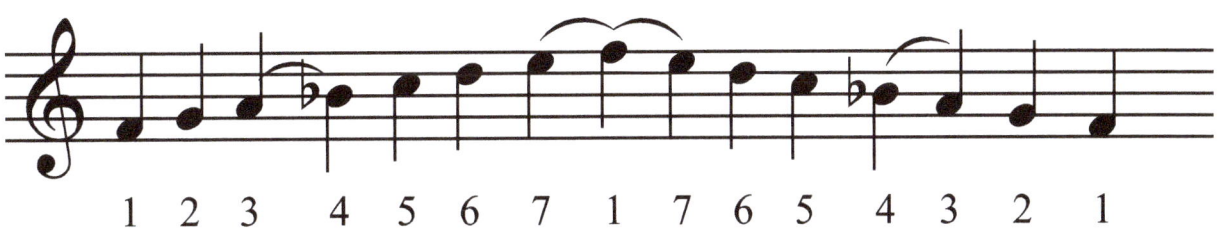

QUESTION 5:

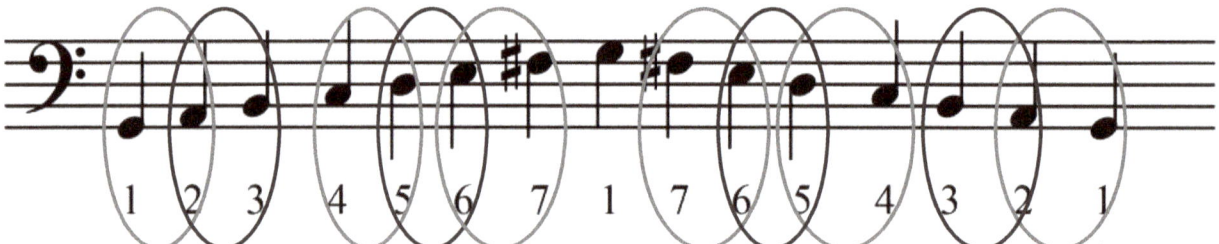

QUESTION 6:

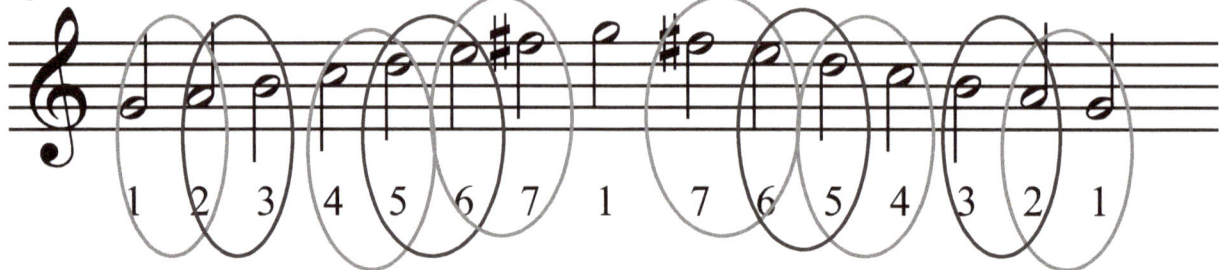

QUESTION 7:

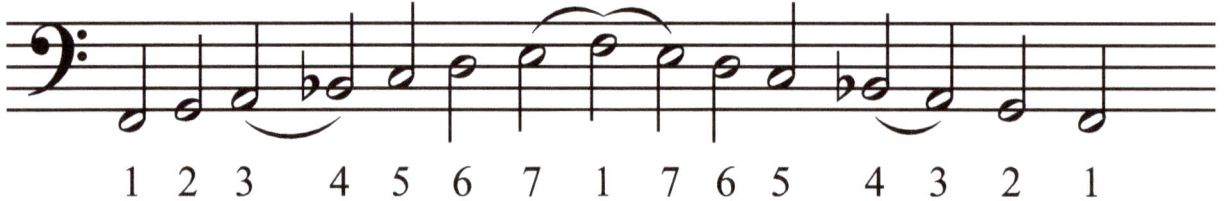

QUESTION 8:

Treble: A G E flat D F sharp F natural E D C A G A F B C E

QUESTION 9:

Sample Answer

QUESTION 10:

Title Those Were The Days	Composer Boris Fomin	Link https://www.youtube.com/watch?v=ozCoq4osSwk

What is the pitch of the melody?	High
What is the melodic contour (shape) of the melody?	Smooth
Does the melody move by steps or leaps, does it move up or down?	Steps up and down
Is the overall tonality major, minor, modal? Is there a change of key?	Minor

MELODY: An organised sequence of single notes.

TONALITY	What scale is used? ☐ Major ☑ **Minor** ☐ Blues ☐ Other:
STRUCTURE	How many bars in each phrase? ☐ 2 ☑ **4** ☐ 8 ☐ other
	Are the phrases ☑ **arched** ☐ spiky or ☐ a mixture?
	Are the cadences (endings) ☑ **predictable** or ☐ unpredictable?
	Does the melody move by ☑ **step (conjunct)**
	☐ skip (broken chord based) ☐ leap (disjunct) ☐ chromatically or ☐ a mixture
	If a song, is it ☑ **strophic (verse/chorus)** or ☐ through-composed?
	Is there any ☐ repetition or ☐ imitation?
STYLE	Does the melody have ☑ **vocal (easy to sing)** or ☐ instrumental origins?
	What is the style? ☐ Jazz ☐ Rock ☐ Movie ☑ **Folk** ☐ Other

HARMONY: The simultaneous sound of two or more notes.

TONALITY	Are the chords ☐ major, ☑ **minor** or ☐ a mixture
CHORD PROGRESSIONS	Are the chords ☐ dissonant (clash) or ☑ **consonant (they fit)**?
	Is there a ☐ 12 bar Blues, ☑ **16 bar pattern** or ☐ other?
	Are the cadences (endings) ☑ **perfect (V-I)**
	☑ **imperfect (I-V)** ☐ plagal (IV-I) or ☐ interrupted (V-vi)?
	Is the Harmonic Rhythm (rate of chord changes) ☐ fast ☑ **medium** ☐ slow?
	Are there any modulations (key changes)? ☑ **No** ☐ Yes
	What is the relationship between the old and new keys? _____
	Is there a: ☐ Tierce de Picardie (a major 3rd in the final chord of a minor key)
	☐ drone (sustained part - tonic and dominant) ☐ suspension ☐ ornaments

Lesson 6

QUESTION 1: Name these intervals: 3rd   6th   5th   7th   4th   2nd

QUESTION2:

QUESTION 3:

QUESTION 4:

QUESTION 5:

QUESTION 6:

QUESTION 7:

QUESTION 8:

QUESTION 9:

Sample Answer

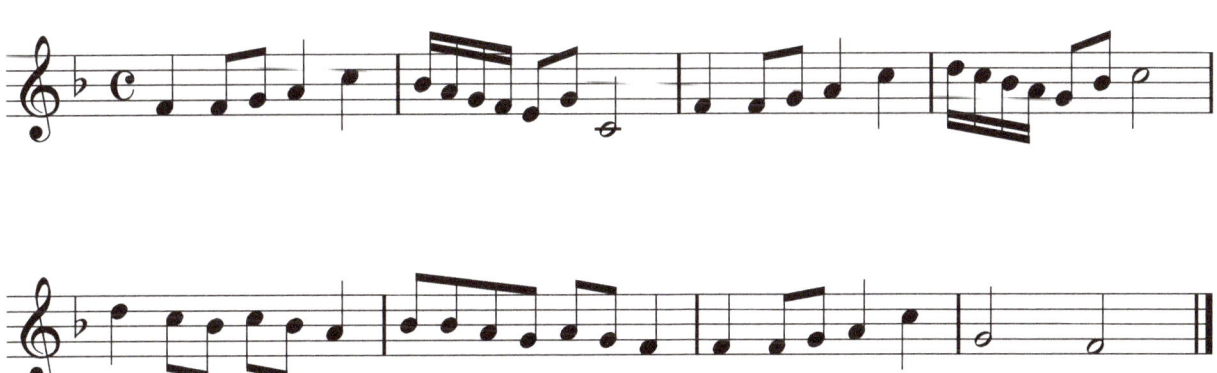

QUESTION 10:

Title 'La Réjouissance' from Fireworks Suite	Composer George Frideric Handel	Link https://www.youtube.com/watch?v=p5jgSVw3nms

What is the pitch of the melody?	High
What is the melodic contour (shape) of the melody?	Smooth
Does the melody move by steps or leaps, does it move up or down?	Mostly by step up and down
Is the overall tonality major, minor, modal? Is there a change of key?	Major

MELODY: An organised sequence of single notes.

TONALITY	What scale is used? ☑ **Major** ☐ Minor ☐ Blues ☐ Other: _____
STRUCTURE	How many bars in each phrase? ☐ 2 ☑ **4** ☐ 8 ☐ other
	Are the phrases ☑ **arched** ☐ spiky or ☐ a mixture?
	Are the cadences *(endings)* ☑ **predictable** or ☐ unpredictable?
	Does the melody move by ☑ **step** *(conjunct)*
	☐ skip *(broken chord based)* ☐ leap *(disjunct)* ☐ chromatically or ☐ a mixture
	If a song, is it ☐ strophic *(verse/chorus)* or ☐ through-composed?
	Is there any ☐ repetition or ☐ imitation?
STYLE	Does the melody have ☐ vocal *(easy to sing)* or ☑ **instrumental origins?**
	What is the style? ☐ Jazz ☐ Rock ☐ Movie ☐ Folk ☑ **Other**

HARMONY: The simultaneous sound of two or more notes.

TONALITY	Are the chords ☑ **major,** ☐ minor or ☐ a mixture
CHORD PROGRESSIONS	Are the chords ☐ dissonant *(clash)* or ☑ **consonant** *(they fit)*?
	Is there a ☐ 12 bar Blues, ☐ 16 bar pattern or ☑ **other?**
	Are the cadences *(endings)* ☑ **perfect** *(V-I)*
	☑ **imperfect** *(I-V)* ☐ plagal *(IV-I)* or ☐ interrupted *(V-vi)* ?
	Is the Harmonic Rhythm *(rate of chord changes)* ☐ fast ☐ medium ☑ **slow?**
	Are there any modulations *(key changes)*? ☑ **No** ☐ Yes
	What is the relationship between the old and new keys?
	Is there a: ☐ Tierce de Picardie *(a major 3rd in the final chord of a minor key)*
	☐ drone *(sustained part - tonic and dominant)* ☐ suspension ☐ ornaments

Lesson 7

QUESTION 1:

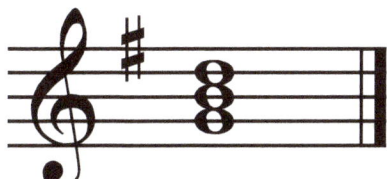  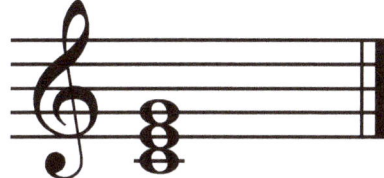

QUESTION 2:

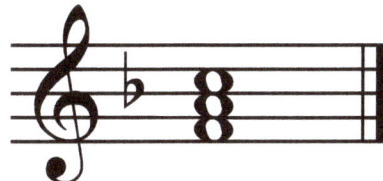  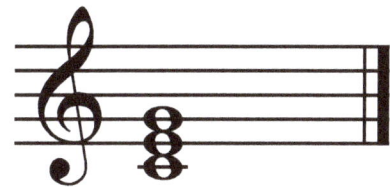

QUESTION 3:

 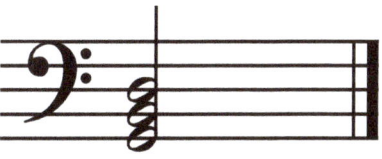 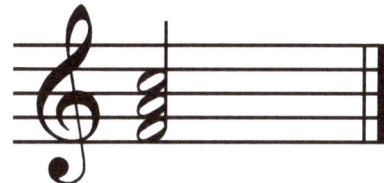

QUESTION 4:

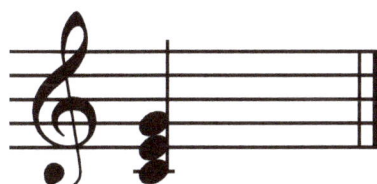  

QUESTION 5:

QUESTION 6

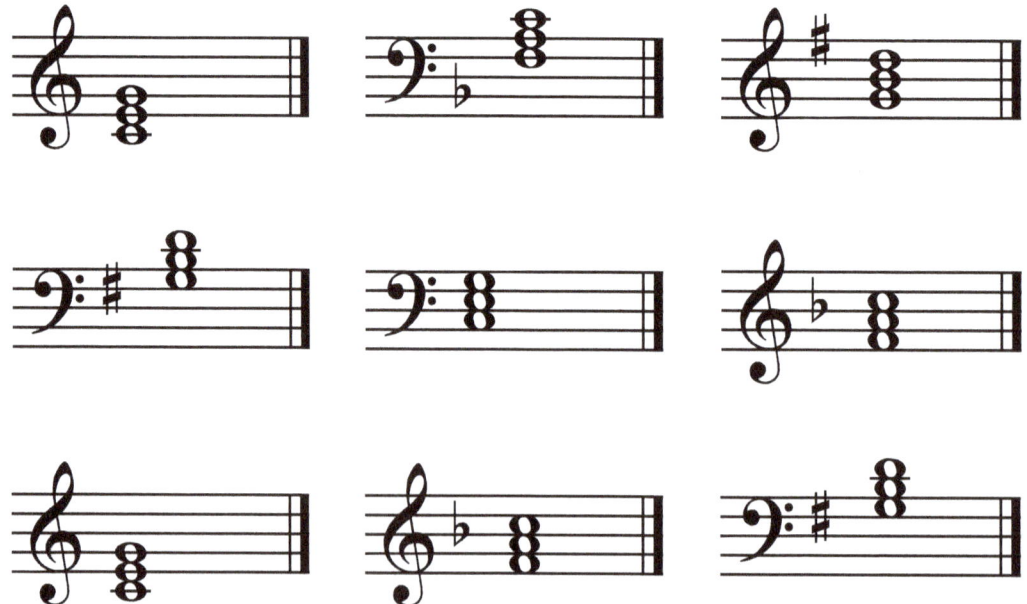

QUESTION 7

Title Altal Mennek	Composer Magyar Roza	Link https://www.youtube.com/watch?v=fDd8w67MPWs

What is the pitch of the melody?	Moderately high
What is the melodic contour (shape) of the melody?	Smooth
Does the melody move by steps or leaps, does it move up or down?	Mainly by steps
Is the overall tonality major, minor, modal? Is there a change of key?	Major

MELODY: An organised sequence of single notes.

TONALITY	What scale is used? ☐ Major ☐ Minor ☐ Blues ☑ Other: Modal
STRUCTURE	How many bars in each phrase? ☐ 2 ☐ 4 ☐ 8
	☑ other 14 bars in each phrase (4+4+4+2)
	Are the phrases ☐ arched ☐ spiky or ☑ a mixture?
	Are the cadences *(endings)* ☑ **predictable** or ☐ unpredictable?
	Does the melody move by ☑ **step** *(conjunct)*
	☐ skip *(broken chord based)* ☐ leap *(disjunct)* ☐ chromatically or ☐ a mixture
	If a song, is it ☐ strophic *(verse/chorus)* or ☐ through-composed?
	Is there any ☐ repetition or ☐ imitation?
STYLE	Does the melody have ☑ **vocal** *(easy to sing)* or ☐ instrumental origins?
	What is the style? ☐ Jazz ☐ Rock ☐ Movie ☑ **Folk** ☐ Other

HARMONY: The simultaneous sound of two or more notes.

TONALITY	Are the chords ☐ major, ☐ minor or ☑ **a mixture**
CHORD PROGRESSIONS	Are the chords ☐ dissonant *(clash)* or ☑ **consonant** *(they fit)*?
	Is there a ☐ 12 bar Blues, ☐ 16 bar pattern or ☑ **other**?
	Are the cadences *(endings)* ☑ **perfect** *(V-I)*
	☑ **imperfect** *(I-V)* ☐ plagal *(IV-I)* or ☐ interrupted *(V-vi)* ?
	Is the Harmonic Rhythm *(rate of chord changes)* ☐ fast ☑ **medium** ☐ slow?
	Are there any modulations *(key changes)*? ☑ **No** ☐ Yes
	What is the relationship between the old and new keys?
	Is there a: ☐ Tierce de Picardie *(a major 3rd in the final chord of a minor key)*
	☐ drone *(sustained part - tonic and dominant)* ☐ suspension ☐ ornaments

Lesson 8

QUESTION 1:

QUESTION 2:

QUESTION 3:

QUESTION 4:

QUESTION 5:

QUESTION 6:

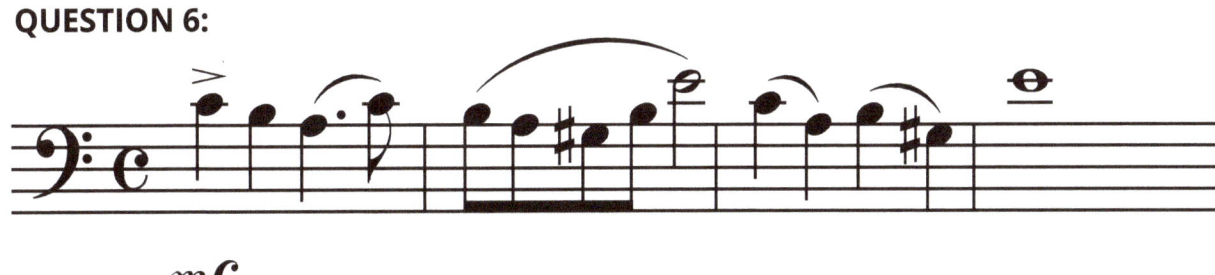

QUESTION 7:

ACCELERANDO	Gradually becoming faster
ACCENT	The note is to be louder, with more attack
ADAGIO	Slowly
BAR	Music is divided by bar lines into these
BASS	Symbol for low sounds
CANTABILE	Lyrically, in a singing style
DIMINUENDO	Gradually becoming softer
FERMATA	Pause; lengthen the value of the note or rest
FIFTH	An interval of seven semitones between two notes
FINE	The end of the piece
FLAT	Lowers a note by one semitone
FORTISSIMO	Very loud
KEY	The major or minor scale around which a piece of music revolves
MINIM	A half note
NATURAL	Cancels a previous sharp or flat
OCTAVE	The difference in pitch between the first and last notes in a music scale
OPUS	A work or group of works
PIANISSIMO	Very softly
QUADRUPLE	Four
RALLENTANDO	Gradually becoming slower
REST	Silence
SEMIBREVE	A whole note
SEMITONE	The distance between one note and the very next

Grade 1 Music Theory Untangled Course Answers

Lesson 9

1) Lively and Fast   2) Soft   3) 8   4) Rallentando   5) 2   6) Yes   7) Yes
8) Loud   9) Legato then staccato   10) Gradually becoming slower

QUESTION 11:

ACROSS
2. Bar: music is divided by bar lines into these
7. Triad: three notes played at the same time
9. FACE: Order of Treble Clef spaces
10. Legato: Smoothly
12. Staccato: Short and detached
15. Coda: A section of music added at the end
16. Cantabile: In a singing style
21. Semibreve: A whole note
22. Repeat: Play again
23. Accent: With attack
24. Forte: Loud
26. Fermata: Pause
28. Natural: Cancels a sharp or flat
30. Fine: The end of a piece
31. Tenuto: Held
33. Leger: Extra lines to extend the staff
34. Sharp: Moves a note up a semitone

DOWN
1. Presto: Very fast
3. Rest: Symbol for silence
4. Adagio: Slowly
5. Common: Another name for Simple Quadruple
6. Bass: Symbol for low sounds
8. Dynamics: Volumes of music
11. Piano: Soft
13. Crescendo: Get louder
14. Allegro: Lively and fast
17. Accelerando: Get faster
18. Flat: Moves a note down a semitone
19. Ritenuto: Slower
20. Mezzo: Moderately
23. ACEG: Order of Bass Clef spaces
25. Staff: Lines and spaces on which music is written
27. Melody: The tune
29. Treble: Symbol for high sounds
32. Tempo: The speed of music

CERTIFICATE
OF COMPLETION

Congratulations on completing

GRADE 1
Music Theory
UNTANGLED COURSE

Jane Stavrinoudis
SIGNED

Jane Stavrinoudis is a distinguished composer, piano teacher, theory expert, and piano examiner whose dedication to music education has spanned many years. Based in Brisbane, Australia, and with a global online presence, Jane has become a cherished mentor for piano teachers and students alike.

For those seeking to enhance their piano skills or delve into music theory, and for teachers looking to develop the techniques, strategies, and insights necessary to inspire students and maximise teaching effectiveness based current best practice and pedagogical approaches, *Jane Stavrinoudis Piano* offers a wealth of resources.
Subscribe to her YouTube channel or visit her website for the latest updates and access to a treasure trove of theory insights and piano sheet music.

Beginner Piano Courses
minidigit Beginner Piano Course (for 5-8 year olds) *OR*
MidiDigits Beginner Piano Course (for 9-12 year olds) *OR*
MaxiDigits Beginner Piano Course (teens to adults)
SavvyDigits Follow on Piano Course (follows on from minidigits, MidiDigits *OR* MaxiDigits)

Music Theory Courses
Grade 1 Music Theory Untangled Course
Grade 2 Music Theory Untangled Course
Grade 3 Music Theory Untangled Course

Piano Sheet Music
Digital downloads of individual pieces in a range of styles from traditional, western and modern. Each download includes a black and white pdf, a colour coded pdf for reluctant music readers, and a short history and analysis of the piece as well as a link to a YouTube demonstration and/or backing video.

Planners
My Student Planner (for instrumental music students)
My Personal Planner (a music-themed personal planner for all ages)
My Mega-Planner (for music teachers: a combination of *My Student Planner* and *My Personal Planner* along with additional sheets for lesson organisation and activities.

BY JANE STAVRINOUDIS

Grade 1 Music Theory Untangled Course
© 2024 Jane Stavrinoudis. All rights reserved. Unauthorised reproduction is illegal. For more courses and piano sheet music visit the website and subscribe to the YouTube channel for Jane Stavrinoudis Piano

www.ingramcontent.com/pod-product-compliance
Lightning Source LLC
Chambersburg PA
CBHW061113070526
44583CB00027B/3277